Food from the Wild

P|

G000162481

Contents

Introduction

Britain's wealth, Maynard Keynes said at the beginning of the last war, lay in her hedges. No country could be poor with hedges like those and by virtue of them Britain was a rich country and could therefore certainly afford to fight a long and expensive war—a statement which still holds today even though inroads by insecticides and over-zealous trimming by county councils have depleted much of the stock. No longer can an abundance of cowslips be taken for granted—they have almost been picked out of existence and are mainly to be found on a few inaccessible railway and motorway embankments—and a plethora of orchids are a thing of the past. But there is still enough to satisfy the curious ; the ones who are prepared to stop, walk, look and pick and not rush by in their cars on their way to supermarkets,

leaving the flowers to pass in a blur seen through the window. Although we eat a great variety of foods today, their variety is made up largely of foreign imports. We actually eat a smaller amount of indigenous produce. Our forbears were far more imaginative and no less health-conscious than ourselves. There is evidence of well over two hundred plants having been eaten in various ways and almost all are attributed with some health-giving factor.

Lack of space in this book makes it impossible to describe all the wild produce there is to eat in Britain, so I have tried to include just that which is reasonably common, will be familiar to most, and which grows in accessible places. On the whole, too, it is produce which has proved its capacity for survival against all attempts at devastation by the human race. So, with a few exceptions, taking enough for yourself need not cause your conscience to worry that you might be

ating today at the expense of those tomorrow.

Another factor which always hovers in the background today is the legislation with which property and wild produce are hedged about. Farmers are within their rights to turn you off their land, so stick to rights of way and footpaths—there are many, all marked on Ordnance Survey maps. Legally, seaweeds, fungi, nuts and molluscs are free for all at any time and so are wild plants which do not fall under the Conservation of Wild Plants Act of 1975. But, with extinction always around the corner, overpicking of anything should always be avoided. The law covering animals, birds and fish is not so simple. Except for vermin, which includes the grey squirrel, rabbits, rats and pigeons (but even with these you must have authorisation to be on the land), the fishing and sporting rights invariably belong to someone and permission from that person must be sought before setting forth with rod and line or gun.

Secondly, most animals and fish are protected by law during their breeding season or 'close season'. This varies with the species but lasts approximately from December to August. There are legal restrictions over the methods you are allowed to use to catch certain animals, birds and fish. To be safe, unless you are adept at tickling trout, which few except gypsies brought up to it are, use a rod and line for fish and a gun (for which you will need a licence) for animals and birds. Gypsies rely on nets, snares and a well-trained lurcher dog for rabbits, hares and even pheasants and partridge but a 12-bore shot-gun, or, for more accuracy, a .22 rifle is easier and more humane. A .275 rifle should be used for deer but should not be fired within fifty yards of a public highway or without a licence.

Finally, always be sure of what you are eating or you may end up dying rather than living off the land.

Leaves

Sorrel *Rumex acetosa*

Common all over Britain but especially in damp meadows, hedgerows and open woodland, sorrel, a relation of the dock, has similar little red flowers which bloom in May and June but smaller, arrow-shaped leaves. The French think so highly of sorrel that they cultivate it and all the best recipes for it come from France. The variety which grows wild in Britain is slightly different, more acid in taste, but also delicious and it can be used in all the same ways. The leaves can be added to salads, used as a sandwich filling or chewed as thirst quenchers as they used to be by country people. The mower in Tolstoy's *Anna Karenina* 'plucked a sorrel stalk and ate it' and in John Clare's *Shepherd's Calendar* 'the mower gladly chews it down, and slakes his thirst the best he may'. Sorrel leaves make an excellent soup and a purée which can be used as an omelette filling or a sauce. Traditionally served with goose or pork, rather bland meats like veal and sweetbread also benefit from its sharp taste. If eaten with fish such as mackerel and shad, it cuts the oiliness.

Green Sauce (to accompany cold meat)

Take a handful of sorrel leaves. Strip off any tough stalks, sprinkle with sugar and chop finely. Put in a jug and pour over 1 tablespoon boiling water, stir, then add enough vinegar to dilute.

Sorrel Purée

Remove any tough stalks from a couple of handfuls of sorrel leaves. Melt a knob of butter in a pan and add the sorrel leaves, stir until they have dissolved in a mush. Add 1 teaspoon flour and then some cream. Heat until it boils and stir into a purée.

Sorrel Soup

To the purée made as above add 825ml ($1\frac{1}{2}$pt) stock or half stock and half milk. Reheat, stirring all the time, and serve hot.

Chickweed *Stellaria media*

Tasting as fresh as young pea-pods, the leaves of chickweed can be boiled, as you would spinach, for a vegetable or

Sorrel

arlic mustard

smell and taste distinctly of garlic. A few leaves or many, according to taste, give zest to a salad and make an excellent filling for sandwiches. Boiled hedge garlic is a Welsh speciality, eaten with fried bacon and herrings. One of the first plants to appear in spring, it is commonly found in hedgerows, has triangular, toothed leaves and heads of white cruciferous flowers from April to June.

Common Mallow
Malva sylvestris

Mallow is reasonably common on roadsides and waste places throughout Britain but more so in the south than the north. It has showy purple to pink flowers, which bloom from June to September, and grows to a height of about 2–3ft. The young furry leaves if picked and boiled make a wholesome although not particularly delicious vegetable, because of the glutinous substances in the leaves. A better way of preparing mallow is to make the leaves into soup. This is a common method of preparation in Egypt, where each family has its own personal recipe. Here is a version suitable for British kitchens :

Mallow Soup

Take 450g (1 lb) leaves and, discarding the stalks, chop them and boil in about 1.1 l (2pt) stock for 10 minutes. Make a sauce by gently frying 2 crushed cloves of garlic in some oil and adding 1 dessertspoon of ground coriander, salt and pepper. Add the stock and simmer the whole mixture for a few minutes, stirring occasionally. Serve the soup by itself or add meat and vegetables.

aten raw as salad. Although hickweed grows in profusion on aste and cultivated ground and is asily collected, it is laborious to repare. The stalks are too stringy to ake pleasant eating and separating e small leaves from them is a time-onsuming business. However, since hickweed is common and grows most the whole year round, it is a egetable source which can always be lied on. The small, white, star-shaped owers close up at night and at the pproach of rain, and bloom ntinuously.

arlic Mustard
lliaria petiolata

well-named plant as its leaves do

Leaves

Ground Elder
Aegopodium podagraria

Although considered one of the most troublesome garden weeds, ground elder is actually just sticking persistently to the place where it was originally planted. It was first grown by monks in medieval monasteries to· be eaten as a cure for gout, hence its other names of goutweed, herb gerard, after the patron saint of gout, and bishop's weed, probably because of its monastic association. Boiled, it makes a parsley-flavoured green vegetable but it can be eaten raw as salad, too. Thickets of the plant will be found in any shady place in or out of the garden. It has elder-shaped leaves, the reason for its name of ground elder, and creamy-white umbelliferous flowers in May and June.

Cow Parsnip
Heracleum sphondylium

A most useful leaf as it grows in bulk, is easily gathered and makes a nourishing, if rather rough-tasting, food. The leaves are best boiled as a green vegetable or made into soup using the recipe for nettle soup. The name hogweed comes from its former use as fodder for pigs ; the alternative, cow parsnip, was given for no apparent reason by William Turner in 1548. A relation of cow parsley, hogweed has larger, looser umbels of white flowers from June to September and larger leaves. It is found in clearings and grassland all over Britain.

Ground elder

Nettle *Uritica dioica*

Three dinners of nettles in April and May were believed by country people to be necessary to purify the blood— and, after a winter's diet consisting of salt meat and very few vegetables, it probably was. Analysis has shown nettles to be the most nutritious of all wild vegetables ; no wild plant exceeds the nettle in its content of nutritive salts and vitamins. Quite apart from this, when eaten young, nettles can make a succulent and tasty vegetable, soup, pudding or stuffing. Levin, on a hunting expedition in *Anna Karenina*, told his servant to draw the birds and stuff them with nettles.

Just the top two whorls of leaves from each plant should be picked, well before the plant begins to flower in

June as, after this, they become gritty and inedible. Wear gloves to avoid being stung. The sting, which comes from formic acid contained in the hairs liberally covering the whole plant, is nullified by heat.

Scotch Nettle Pudding

To 4.5l (1gal) young nettle tops, thoroughly washed, add 2 good-sized leeks or onions, two heads of broccoli or a small cabbage, and 100g ($\frac{1}{4}$lb) rice. Clean the vegetables well, chop the broccoli and leeks and mix with the nettles. Place all together in a muslin bag in alternate layers with the rice, and tie tightly. Boil in salted water long enough to cook the vegetables, the time varying according to the tenderness or otherwise of the greens. Serve with gravy or melted butter. *Wild Vegetables and Salads*, Mrs M. Grieve.

Soup

Sweat 1 large diced potato and a chopped onion in butter until the onion is transparent. Add 2 good handfuls of nettles and 550ml (1pt) stock. Simmer for 20 minutes. Put through a vegetable mill or blender. Add 275ml ($\frac{1}{2}$pt) milk, adjust seasoning, reheat and serve.

Vegetable

Put some washed nettle tops in a pan of boiling salted water. Cook for 5 minutes, drain, add salt, pepper and butter and chop all together over a low heat. Serve.

Dandelion
Taraxacum officinale

Dandelion leaves are best when eaten as salad and, unless blanched, pick only the young inner leaves of the plant. If the plant is blanched, all the leaves are edible. This can be done in two ways : either place a pot over a growing plant as you would for rhubarb, or bank the plant up with earth as for celery. A way of ensuring a supply of winter salad is to dig the roots in autumn, place them in earth in a covered box, leave them under the kitchen table or in a dark cupboard where they will sprout pale, sweet-tasting leaves. The roots are edible too (see page 13). Dandelions are too common to require description ; they grow anywhere and everywhere, and are cultivated by the French who give them the country name of *pis-en-lit* owing to the diuretic effect of the leaves.

Fat Hen *Chenopodium album*

'Boil Myles in water and chop them in butter and you will have a good dish' is an old English saying describing the best way of eating this wholesome leaf which contains more iron, protein, calcium and vitamin B than cabbage. Fat hen formed part of the last meal of Tollund Man, a fact revealed when the contents of his stomach were examined, after he was dug from his Bronze Age grave in the Sussex Marshes near Rye. It was also eaten by the Indians of New Mexico and Arizona. It is found in waste places and cultivated ground and has a liking for manure heaps. Fat hen grows to about 1m (3ft), has lance-shaped leaves and tiny, greenish flowers which bloom between July and October.

Leaves

Bistort *Polygonum bistorta*

The leaves are the main ingredient of a herb pudding formerly served with veal and bacon. Eaten by people in the north-west of England at Easter, it is to this period of the calendar that most of its other names refer—Easter ledges, Easter mangiants and Passion dock. The brush-like head of small pink and white flowers can be seen covering moist meadows on siliceous soils particularly in the north of England from June to August. This is after the traditional time for eating the leaves although it is still possible to cook them now. They can be boiled as a vegetable as well as made into pudding.

Easter Ledger Pudding

Pick young bistort leaves, dandelion, lady's mantle, or nettle and submerge in boiling water for 20 minutes. Strain and chop. To the mixture add a little boiled barley, a chopped hard-boiled egg, butter, pepper and salt and heat in a saucepan. Press into a pudding basin to shape. Serve with veal and bacon.

Watercress
Nasturtium officinale

Full of valuable, nutritive mineral oils, watercress can also be very polluted, since it is largely composed of the water it grows in. It can even be poisonous. Careful notice should therefore be taken of the habitat of the cress you are picking. Common in running water, it bears small white flowers between May and October.

Wild cress is usually stronger than the garden variety and was valued as a scurvy preventative and thought to promote the appetite when eaten as salad. The Romans ate it with vinegar as a cure for mental complaints. Besides salad, watercress also makes a delicious soup.

Watercress Soup

'Melt a large lump of butter in a saucepan and add chopped spring onions or shallots, garlic, root ginger (optional) and stir over a low heat for a few minutes. Add watercress, raise the heat and cook until the watercress has softened. Add salt and pepper, some marjoram and chicken stock. Bring to the boil, then liquidise. Reheat and serve.' Suki Kinloch.

Yarrow *Achillea millefolium*

Aromatic and coarse textured, the ferny leaves of yarrow are most

Yarrow

Wild Cabbage

persistent, making inroads even into
Hyde Park in London. Finely chopped,
the leaves are often used as a substitute
for chervil to add pungency to a salad
or, if picked during a walk, they can
provide a satisfying stopgap for
hunger. Yarrow leaves used to be taken
as snuff from which they acquired the
name Old Man's Pepper. Yarrow has
bunches of small white and pink
flowers which bloom from June to
August.

Wild Cabbage
Brassica oleracea

All domestic cabbages, Brussels
sprouts, and broccoli are derived from
the wild cabbage though probably
from continental rather than British
stock. Selective breeding started early :
Pliny distinguishes between wild and
domestic cabbage in his *Natural
History*, though originally all cabbage
was grown for medicinal rather than

vegetative purposes. Wild cabbage has
few of the outward appearances of the
domestic cabbage ; a loose bunch of
rather acrid-tasting leaves, they are
best boiled or casseroled in the same
way as the domestic variety but for a
longer time as thorough cooking is
necessary to remove the bitterness.
Not particularly common, the wild
cabbage grows on sea cliffs in the
south of England and Wales, has large
grey leaves and yellow cruciferous
flowers. These are easily confused
with those of charlock, mustard,
turnip and rape, all of which grow
wild but mostly on arable ground and
have good-sized, thoroughly edible
leaves. Charlock in particular was
often eaten by the Hebridean islanders.
The broad stalks were usually stripped
from the leaves and cooked separately.
It was also popular in Ireland and used
to be sold in Dublin street markets
during the eighteenth century.

Stems

Hop *Humulus lupulus*

The young shoots of the hop are picked when they appear in spring, tied in bundles, as with asparagus, and boiled for about 20 minutes. They make an excellent spring vegetable. Once appreciated by the Romans, Pliny mentions their cultivation for this purpose. Hop shoots were also sold in English markets. They are found climbing through hedges in many parts of Britain.

Lovage *Ligusticum scoticum*

If earthed up and blanched, the stalks of lovage resemble celery, but are inferior in flavour. As its Latin name suggests, lovage is a Scottish speciality ; it doesn't grow south of Northumberland and prefers a coastal habitat. A tall plant growing to 1 m (3ft), it has large, glossy leaves, red stalks and greenish-coloured flowers which bloom in June and July.

Elder *Sambucus nigra*

In mid-April the young shoots of new growth on elder trees should have attained optimum size for eating. Peel the pith off, then tie in bundles and boil for about 20 minutes. Another way of using them is to pickle them. Use the recipe for ash keys on page 24. The elder is a common hedgerow tree with many other uses (see Berries, and Flowers).

Sea-kale *Crambe maritima*

Miller in his *Gardener's Dictionary* of 1731 says that 'the inhabitants (of Sussex) gather it in the spring to eat,

Sea-kale

preferring it to any of the Cabbage kind.' Previously it was common to blanch the stems by piling up pebbles from the beach around the growing plants. Then bunches were picked and taken to local markets for sale. The stems were separated from the tough leaves and eaten either chopped and raw in salads or cooked, preferably by steaming, and served with butter or in a cheese sauce. The leaves should be cooked like spinach.

Samphire *Crithmum maritimum*

At one time samphire was popular enough for it to be sold in London markets under the cry of 'Crest Marine'. But by the middle of the seventeenth century, Culpeper was bewailing its lack of popularity and the foolishness of the people who no longer ate this plant valuable for all 'ill digestion and obstructions' that 'are the cause of most of the diseases which the frail nature of man is subject to'. However, the habit of eating it never quite died out in Norfolk and other coastal areas with shingly shores. This is where samphire proliferates from June to September; it is considered to be in its prime during the first two weeks of July. The stem, although inclined to be stringy, is full of spicy juice and the leaves are thick and succulent. They can be eaten raw as salad, or boiled and served, hot with butter, or cold with bread and butter for a Yorkshire speciality.

This recipe, given by John Evelyn in his *Acetaria* of 1699, makes what Gerard considered 'the pleasantest sauce':

'Let it be gathered about Michaelmas or in the spring and put two or three hours into a brine of water and salt, then into a clean tinned brass pot with three parts of strong white vinegar and one part of water and salt or as much as will cover the sampier, keeping the vapour from issuing out by pushing down the pot lid, and so hang it over the fire for half an hour only. Being taken off let it remain cover'd till it be cold and then put it up into small barrels or jars with the liquor and some fresh vinegar, water and salt, and thus it will keep very green. If you be near the sea that water will supply the place of brine. This is a Dover Receit.'

Thistle *Cirsium eriophorum; Onopordum acanthium*

The young stems, when stripped of their rind, can be boiled and eaten while the bracts of the flowers were eaten in former times in the same way as artichokes. Although most thistles can be treated and eaten in this way, obviously it is more profitable to concentrate on the larger varieties, particularly the woolly thistle (*Cirsium eriophorum*) and the Scotch thistle (*Onopordum acanthium*). Getting past the fearsome spines is made easier if the stalk is put in boiling water for 1 minute before attempting to peel it.

Samphire

11

Roots

Horse-radish
Armoracia rusticana

Introduced into the UK in the sixteenth century, probably from Germany, it was initially eaten as a cure for worms and coughs. But by 1597 its fame as a sauce had reached Gerard who remarked that it 'is commonly used among the Germans for sauce to eate fish with and such like meates as we do mustarde'; and by 1657 a taste for the sauce had gained ground here because Cole states that 'the root, sliced thin and mixed with vinegar is eaten as a sauce with meat, as among the Germans'. The yellow tap-root may be traced by its docklike leaves and spike of white cruciferous flowers in May and June.

Horse-radish

Horse-radish Sauce

Grate 2 tablespoons horse-radish and add it to $\frac{1}{2}$ teaspoon made mustard, 1 dessertspoon white wine vinegar, sugar to taste and salt and pepper. Mix all together, then add 140ml ($\frac{1}{4}$pt) of whipped cream slowly. Chill and serve.

Cuckoo-pint *Arum maculatum*

Although every part of the cuckoo-pint which grows above ground is poisonous, below, the small, potato-like root is perfectly edible. Full of nutritious starch it makes a good vegetable. After digging, the root should first be allowed to dry out before being cooked by boiling or baking. Portland sago or Portland arrowroot was made from the dried ground roots of cuckoo-pint. A southern woodland plant, the leaves, often spotted, appear in January followed by the yellow spadix in May. The suggestive shape of the latter led to the idea that the plant had aphrodisiac qualities. 'They have eaten so much Wake Robin' (as cuckoo-pint used to be known) 'that they cannot sleep for love' wrote John Lyly in his play *Loves Metamorphosis* in 1601.

Dandelion *Taraxacum officinale*

The best known way of eating the roots is as dandelion coffee. This is a non-caffeinated coffee which tastes surprisingly like the real thing. The roots should be dug in autumn, washed (laying them in a string bag under running water is an easy way) then dried, roasted in the oven and finally ground. To make coffee simply put some of the grounds in a jug, pour on boiling water, allow to stand for a few minutes and pour out through a strainer.

To eat dandelion roots as a vegetable, dig and wash, then peel and scrub

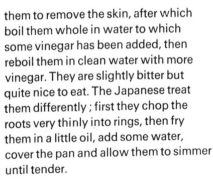

Cuckoo-pint

Silverweed

them to remove the skin, after which boil them whole in water to which some vinegar has been added, then reboil them in clean water with more vinegar. They are slightly bitter but quite nice to eat. The Japanese treat them differently ; first they chop the roots very thinly into rings, then fry them in a little oil, add some water, cover the pan and allow them to simmer until tender.

Earthnut

The small, edible bulbs lie 5–7cm (2–3in) below ground attached to their green ferny leaves and white umbels by a white, thread-like stem. This has to be followed carefully underground—it breaks easily—to its root source. The small, nutty-tasting bulb is then unearthed, scraped and cleaned before eating. The best instrument to use for this operation is a penknife, though Caliban in *The Tempest* used his finger-nails. Nicest

raw, earthnuts may also be boiled, baked or put in soups and stews.

Silverweed *Potentilla anserina*

The roots, tasting like parsnips, can be dried and milled into flour, coarsely ground and made into porridge, eaten raw, boiled, baked or added to soups and stews. Until the advent of potatoes, silverweed roots formed a vital part of the diet of people living in the more northerly, upland areas of Britain, particularly the Hebrides where they are said to have been cultivated as a crop. It must have been hard work. From my experience, silverweed roots are small and awkward to dig. There would have been no difficulty in finding them, however, as the yellow flowers and grey-green, cut-edged leaves grow anywhere up to a height of 526m (1,400ft). Silverweed has an insidious, creeping, root stock and blooms from May to August.

Flowers

Chamomile *Anthemis nobilis*

'It hath floures wonderfully shynynge yellow and resemblynge the appell of an eye' eulogised Turner of the chamomile. As the petals begin to droop, pick the flower heads and dry them by spreading them out on trays in a cool, airy place turning them occasionally. A tea can then be made of the shrivelled flowers. Pour boiling water on to a teaspoonful and allow to infuse for 5–10 minutes before straining into a cup.

Elder *Sambucus nigra*

The flowers, with their strong, honey-like scent, flavour anything they are put in contact with. A spray of fresh elder flowers infused in boiling water makes a tea, or put in vinegar will make elder flower vinegar. They were often used to flavour custards and creams and dipped in batter and fried for elder flower fritters. Elder flower champagne and cordial are well known and as a cooling summer drink the latter is unsurpassed.

Elder Flower Cordial

'Dissolve 2.3kg (5lb) sugar in 2.75l (5pt) water and when hot add 50g (2oz) citric acid (to be bought from most chemists) and pour over 900g (2lb) of elder flowers with the worst of their stalks removed. Stir and press down well. Cover and leave for 24 hours. Bottle. To drink, dilute with water and add ice.' Kate ter Horst.

Eyebright *Euphrasia nemorosa*

Fresh, the whole plant, flowers and all, can be used for making wine (use the recipe for dandelion on p.15). Dried, it makes an excellent tea and one which used to be given to people suffering from afflictions of the eye— hence the herb's name. 'The purple and yellow spots and stripes which are upon the flowers of the Eyebright doth very much resemble the diseases of the eye, as bloodshot, etc., by which signature it hath been found out that this herb is effectual for curing the same'. Culpeper said that 'if the herb was but as much used as it is neglected, it would half spoil the spectacle maker's trade.' A little, tufted plant with hairy leaves and delicate flowers, it is common on wasteland and grassland throughout Britain.

Heather *Erica*

'Boethius records that from the honeyed flowers of the purple heather the Picts made a sweet beer, the secret of its compounding being hereditary in the tribe, and never revealed to an alien even under threat of death. This may have been the cup which Rowena gave to Hengist'. *Flowers as Food*, Florence White.

Heather Ale

For 9l (2gal) heather ale, gather enough flower spikes to fill a 4.5l (1gal) container. Cover with water and boil for 1 hour. Strain and add 25g (1oz) ginger, 4–5 cloves, and 12g ($\frac{1}{2}$oz) hops previously boiled for 20 minutes in 1.1l (2pt) water. This is then strained and 450g (1lb) sugar and 450g (1lb) malt is added and boiled for a few minutes. Allow to cool to blood heat and add 1 teaspoon yeast. Add the 4.5l (1gal) water which the heather shoots were boiled in. Leave to ferment for 2–3 days, then skim off any remaining fermentation, siphon off into bottles, screw down tops and in 21 days you have ale fit for drinking.

Dandelion *Taraxacum officinale*

The flower heads may be made into tea in the same way as camomile or used to make one of the sweetest and best of flower wines.

Dandelion Wine

Put 4.5l (1gal) of dandelion flowers in 4.5l (1gal) of cold water and bring to the boil. Simmer for 10 minutes then strain on to 1.6kg (3½lb) sugar, and the rind of a lemon and orange. Stir well.

When reduced to blood heat, add the juice of the lemon and orange and some yeast which has been previously activated. (If this is bought yeast, there will be instructions on the packet; if bakers' yeast, mix with a little sugar and lukewarm water, spread on toast and float on the top of the wine.) Cover with butter muslin and leave in a warm place for 2 days to start fermenting. Then pour into a jar and either insert an airlock—which can be bought from a wine shop—or plug the jar with cotton wool. Leave until all fermentation has ceased. Siphon off into bottles, cork and keep as long as possible—6 months at the least—before drinking.

Flowers

Gorse *Ulex*

A wine as sweet as the smell of the yellow gorse flowers can be made at almost any time of the year because, as the saying goes, 'When gorse is out of bloom, kissing's out of season' which, of course, it never is. Use the recipe for dandelion wine.

Primrose *Primula vulgaris*

The flowers may be infused for tea, crystallised for decorating cakes or made into a vinegar for which, according to Florence White in *Good Things in England*, the housewives of Wakefield were famous.

Primrose Vinegar

Ingredients : cold water 34l (30qt) ; brown sugar 5.45kg (12lb) ; primroses 9l (1 peck) ; Yeast (compressed yeast, 25–50g, 1–2oz). Time : 10 minutes to boil ; a few days to stand ; a year to mature in the cask. Boil the water and sugar together for 10 minutes. Before it is cold add 9l (1 peck) primrose petals and the yeast creamed with a little sugar. Let it work for a few days, stirring often. Put it in a barrel with the primroses. Keep it in the warmth and let it stand for 1 year.

Rose *Rosa*

Commonly called dogroses, not because of any similarity to the animal, but from 'dag' the old word for thorn. There are many different kinds, but it takes an expert to tell between them. Almost all bloom around June, sprawling across hedgerows all over the country. Their fragile petals never attain the density of smell of their garden relations, but a delicate conserve, wine or syllabub can be made using wild roses or garden varieties.

Rose Wine

Put 2.2l (4pt) rose petals in a bowl and pour over 2.2l (4pt) boiling water. Cover with butter muslin and leave until the water has become thoroughly impregnated with the scent of the roses. Strain through a muslin squeezing out all the liquid from the petals. Place liquid in a pan with 900g (2lb) white sugar and bring slowly to the boil, skimming off any scum which rises. Boil for 10 minutes. Allow to cool to blood heat, then add some previously activated yeast. Pour into a fermentation jar and either insert an airlock or plug with cotton wool. Leave until all fermentation has ceased, then bottle off. Keep for as long as possible before drinking to allow the perfume to develop.

Rose Syllabub

Take the white of a new-laid egg and beat it well. Beat into it conserve of roses until the whole is the consistency of cream.

Conserve of Roses

This recipe is a modernised version of the one given by that great seventeenth century figure, Sir Kennelm Digby : Cut the white ends off 450g (1lb) scented red roses and boil the rest gently in 825ml (1½pt) soft water, keeping the pan covered, until the colour of the roses has bled into the water and they look like pale linen. This will take from 30 minutes to 1 hour. Strain off the liquor, pressing the

petals to make sure that all the flavour, scent and colour is extracted. Set the liquor on a gentle heat and add 450g (1lb) castor sugar and when this is dissolved add a second pound, then a third and finally a fourth. Boil the 1.8kg (4lb) sugar with the rose liquor until it forms a syrup and sets when tested. Remove from the heat and immediately add some more pale-coloured, scented rose petals. Stir well to mix all uniformly. Allow to stand until cool and put in pots. If you put the conserve into pots while it is still quite warm and leave the pots uncovered for some days in the sun or in a warm place, the top of the conserve will crystallise. This will preserve the syrup against mould and paper tops will not be needed. Break the candied crust to take out the conserve as required.

Rose Petal Jelly (for eating as jam) Make an apple jelly in the same way as mint jelly leaving out the mint. Pound scented rose petals (if a modern variety, cut off the white tip of each petal first) in a mortar with a small quantity of castor or loaf sugar. After this, put with a few tablespoons of water in a fireproof dish and leave for 1 hour in a cool oven. The petals may be allowed to reach simmering point but must never boil. When it is apparent that the sugar and water have absorbed the flavour from the petals, strain, add the liquid to the boiling jelly and bring back to the boil. If the flavour is not strong enough, put the petal pulp in a muslin bag and plunge it in the boiling syrup for a few minutes.

Dog rose

Berries

Bilberry *Vaccinium myrtillus*

Except in the very south of England any moor, heath or woodland with an acid soil should have masses of this low bushy plant, often growing amidst heather or boggy grass. The soft, blue, pungent-tasting fruit is ready for picking in August. The berries can be eaten with sugar and cream, or made into puddings and pies, jam or wine. In Switzerland they are distilled into 'schnapps'.

Bilberry Fritters

First make a batter by putting 100g (¼lb) flour with a pinch of salt into a bowl. Make a well in the centre and break in an egg. Gradually incorporate the flour into the egg adding up to 140ml (¼pt) milk or water as the mixture thickens. Beat well and leave to stand for 2 hours before adding enough bilberries to thicken the batter. Heat some butter in a pan and drop in dollops. Turn, drain on paper, dust with castor sugar and serve immediately.

Bilberry Jam

Warm 450g (1lb) ripe bilberries in a pan until the juice runs. Then add 450g (1lb) sugar and bring to the boil. Simmer until the jam is of the right consistency.

Hawthorn
Crataegus monogyna

The berries, though inedible raw, when cooked make a spicy jelly or wine and, if steeped in brandy for a few months, form a fine liquor.

Bilberry

Hawthorn Jelly

Simmer the fruit with some water to release the juice, then strain it through a coarse flannel or fine sieve. To every 550ml (1pt) of juice add 450g (1lb) sugar. Add the juice of a lemon and boil until the mixture sets when tested.

Blackberry *Rubus fruticosus*

A Neolithic man unearthed in Essex had the remains of blackberries in his stomach and Lavinia in Victoria Sackville-West's novel, *All Passion Spent* had 'a passion for getting something for nothing. . . . Every blackberry in the hedgerow was an agony to Lavinia until she had bottled it.' The sweetest blackberries are those which ripen first, at the base of the cluster. After this they ripen progressively up the stalk decreasing in flavour until, in October, they are all seed and fit only for cooking with apples. Jams, puddings, wine, can all be made from blackberries, and recipes for these will be found in many cookery books. Here are two which might not:

Welsh Blackberry and Bread Pudding

Put some blackberries to simmer with just enough water to cover them and throw in torn pieces of bread until most of the liquid is absorbed. Sweeten with sugar and, when the fruit is soft, put into a bowl and allow to cool. Serve with thick cream.

Blackberry Vinegar Drink

Mix equal parts of blackberry juice with cider. Strain and mix in enough honey to float an egg. Simmer for 15 minutes, then cool and put in a barrel or earthenware container. Leave until March before bottling and then for 6 weeks before drinking.

Bullace *Prunus domestica*

The tree, which looks like a blackthorn, has fruit which, though larger and more oval, resembles the sloe. Botanically, bullace is a relation of the domestic plum and the fruit may be used in the same ways as plums or sloes. Too sour to eat raw, they are best cooked and put in pies or made into jam or wine.

Bullace Wine

Pour 4.5l (1gal) of boiling water over 1.8kg (4lb) bullace. Mash and stir in 1.5kg (3½lb) sugar and allow to cool to blood heat before adding some previously activated yeast. Cover and leave to ferment for 3–4 days. Strain into a jar and add 450g (1lb) chopped raisins. Then plug the neck of the jar with cotton wool or put in an airlock. Leave until fermentation has ceased, then bottle.

Berries

Rose Hip *Rosa*

Rose hips contain more vitamin C than any other fruit or vegetable except walnuts, a source made use of by the government during World War II when voluntary collectors gathered an average of 450 tons during 1943–6 for conversion into rose hip syrup. This is a version of the recipe given by the Ministry of Food :

Rose Hip Syrup

Coarsley mince the hips and put *immediately* into 1.65l (3pt) of boiling water. Bring back to the boil, then remove from the heat and leave to stand for 15 minutes. Pour into a flannel or jelly bag and allow to drip until the bulk of the liquid has come through. Return the residue to the saucepan, add 825ml (1½pt) boiling water, stir, allow to stand for 10 minutes. Pour back into jelly bag and leave to drip again. Put both mixtures of juice into a clean saucepan and boil until reduced to 825ml (1½pt). Then add 550g (1¼lb) sugar and boil for another 5 minutes. Pour into sterilised bottles and seal. (Make sure none of the sharp hairs from the hips are in the mixture. Re-strain if in any doubt.)

Raspberry *Rubus idaeus*

Ripe, wild raspberries are so good that any intermediate stage between bush and mouth is really unnecessary. However, a glut may make the mind wander to variations on the theme. If so, the method of cooking should be simple in order not to spoil the flavour. Raspberries grow over a surprisingly wide latitude. They form large bushes in woods and heaths, producing fruit from as early as June in the South until the autumn in the North, from the Middle East to Siberia.

Raspberry Dessert

Sprinkle fresh raspberries with sugar and leave for a few hours for it to steep. Then sprinkle with some wine or brandy before serving with cream.

Raspberry Cream

'When you have whipt your cream, sweeten it, and take two ladlefulls, and bruise the raspberries into it, and season with rosewater, and again whip it well, and then put it to your cream and, stirring all together, dish it up.' (1700 manuscript.)

Elderberry *Sambucus nigra*

A tree which is regarded with great superstition from the belief that Christ was nailed to a cross made of elder. Stories of its associations with the devil and witchcraft would fill a book. Rather an unfair attitude to take about

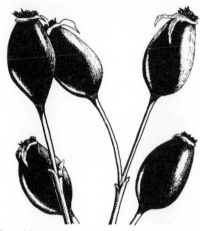

Rose hips

tree of which every part has been used in some way. The berries are no exception. They should not be picked until the clusters have turned upside down ; this shows that they are ripe. ...edible raw and, because of the sharp pip each berry contains, difficult to eat cooked, they are best made into jellies or drinks. Elderberry Rob is a time-honoured cure for colds.

Elderberry Rob

Put about 2.2l (2qt) elderberries into a hot oven and leave until the juice runs, strain off and to each 550ml (1pt) add 200g ($\frac{1}{2}$lb) sugar, $\frac{1}{4}$ teaspoon cinnamon and 12 cloves. Cover and simmer until thick, about 30 minutes. Bottle and cork.

Elderberry Wine

Strip 1.8–2.2kg (4–5lb) berries from their stalks with a fork and pour on 4.5l (1gal) boiling water and allow to stand for 3 days, stirring and mashing the berries each day. Strain into a pan and add 50g (2oz) bruised ginger, 12g ($\frac{1}{2}$oz) cloves, a pinch of allspice and peeled rind of one lemon. Bring to the boil and simmer for 10 minutes. Allow to cool, then add 1.5kg (3$\frac{1}{2}$lb) sugar. Add lemon juice and when the liquid is blood heat, add previously activated yeast. Pour into a fermentation jar, insert an airlock and put in a warm place. When fermentation ceases, bottle off.

Berries

Rowanberry *Sorbus aucuparia*

In northern Europe the berries were dried and ground into flour and in Russia they were steeped in vodka to make rowanberry vodka, as this scene from Pasternak's *Dr Zhivago* shows : 'Beyond the open doors of the ballroom the supper table gleamed, white and long as a winter road. The play of light on frosted bottles of red rowanberry vodka caught the eye.'

Diodgriafel

'Diodgriafel is made of the berries of *Solus Aucuparta* by pouring water over the mashed berries and setting the infusion to ferment. When kept for some time this is by no means an unpleasant liquor. In Scotland a spiritous liquor is obtained by distillation.' Evans, 1798.

Rowan Jelly

Place 2.7kg (6lb) rowanberries, stalked and washed, in a pan with 1.65l (3pt) water. Simmer until the berries are soft. Strain through a muslin bag. Measure the liquid and to every 550ml (1pt) allow 650g (1½lb) sugar. Add the juice of a lemon and boil for about 30 minutes or until the mixture sets when tested.

Sloe *Prunus spinosa*

Sloes, the fruit of the blackthorn tree, should be left until October before picking and have been softened and sweetened by a few frosts. Too sour to eat raw, they are best made into wine or added to gin for sloe gin.

Sloe Wine

Add 1.1l (2pt) boiling water to 1.1l (2pt) sloes and leave for 4 days stirring twice a day. Strain and for each 1.1l (2pt) liquid add 450g (1lb) sugar. Leave for another 4 days stirring every day. Bottle and cork lightly until fermentation has ceased.

Sloe Gin

Put 1.65l (3pt) sloes, 35g (1½oz) bitter almonds, 650g (1½lb) sugar and 2.2l (4pt) gin in a jar and cork. Shake every 3 days for 3 months. Strain off the liquor into bottles, seal and, though it may be drunk now, it will improve with keeping.

Strawberry *Fragaria vesca*

How tastes change. The strawberry, dismissed by Pliny, who said that he knew of two kinds, one growing on the ground and one on a tree but that neither flavour was exciting, is today considered one of the choicest fruits. They should be eaten as soon after picking as possible when the flavour is at its height. Purists dip their strawberries in a little salt, but others prefer sugar and cream. A favourite of the seventeenth century was wine made from strawberries. Here is a recipe :

A Cordial Water of Sir Walter Raleigh

'Take a gallon [4.5l] of Strawberries, and put into them a pinte [550ml] of aqua vitae [brandy], let them stand four or five dayes, strain them gently out, and sweeten the water as you please with fine sugar, or else with perfume [probably rose water].' W.M. (cook to Queen Henrietta

Maria), *The Queen's Closet Opened*, 1655.

Apple *Malus*

Wild apples, either the indigenous crab apple or a self-seeded domestic apple are common over the whole of Britain with the exception of the north of Scotland. Though most frequently found in oak woods, the best and largest fruit comes from trees growing in hedgerows where there is more light. Wild apples never grow as large or as sweet as domestic ones and need to be cooked with sugar in order to be palatable. Previously, every farmhouse had an orchard stocked with sweet apples for eating, acid ones for cooking and extremely acid ones for making cider and ver juice—an astringent vinegar used like lemon. Ways of cooking apples are numerous and every cook book has recipes.

Apple Drink

This is a modernised version of a recipe given in the *Closet of the Emminently learned Sir Kennelm Digby Opened* (1669) :

Slice about 1.3kg (3lb) apples and boil them in about 2.2l (4pt) water for 10–15 minutes or until the water and the apples have formed a mush. Sweeten with sugar or honey to your taste. Bottle, cork and leave for 3 months. A thick mould will form on the top which should be removed before drinking. The rest of the juice will be clear and more delicious than any cider. A little rosemary, added to the apples when they are cooking, and a curl of lemon peel, put in each bottle when bottling will make the flavour even better.

Seeds

Ash *Fraxinus excelsior*

The familiar 'keys', which contain the seeds of the tree, can be made into a pickle. Evelyn recommends this as 'having the virtue of capers' and the frequency with which recipes for pickled ash keys appear in old cookery books testifies to their common use at table. They should be picked young, before August, after which they become too tough.

Pickle

Boil the keys in water twice, using fresh water for the second boiling. Then place the keys in a jar and cover with hot, spiced vinegar.

Caraway *Carum carvi*

Though not particularly common, the caraway plant will grow anywhere. It looks like cow parsley and the lacy flowers bloom in June and July. Once the fruits are fully developed, they should be collected, and threshed to separate the seeds. These should then be dried in the sun or a warm place, and shaken or turned over occasionally. They can be used to flavour cakes, bread, cheese, soups and cabbage. The basic taste of the liqueur kümmel is oil of caraway, pressed from the seeds and 'a pippin and a dish of caraways' was eaten as a condiment by Falstaff in *Henry V*, at Trinity College Cambridge and at city livery dinners too.

Seed Cake

Take 4 eggs and their weight in butter, sugar and flour, $\frac{1}{2}$ teaspoon baking powder, 1 dessertspoon cornflour, 1 teaspoon caraway seeds. Sieve together the flour, cornflour and baking powder. Add the caraway seeds. Cream the butter and sugar and add the eggs. Gradually fold in the flours. Mix thoroughly, put in a buttered tin and bake in a hot oven.

Mustard *Brassica nigra; Sinapsis alba*

The 'seede of Mustard pounded with vinegar is an excellent sauce, good to be eaten with any grosse meates, either fish or flesh, because it doe help the digestion, warmeth the stomache and provoketh appetite' said Gerard. Until about 1720 when Mrs Clements of Durham invented what we now know as powdered mustard, the seeds were more often used whole as a pickling spice, or pounded and made up into balls with honey or vinegar and other spices. Gerard recommended that you steep a mixture of mustard seed overnight in vinegar, pound it in the morning with more vinegar and add spices, wine or honey to taste. For all mustards both black and white seeds are used with a higher proportion of black. Black mustard is indigenous to cliffs in the south-west of England and is found by streams and waste places elsewhere. White mustard is a naturalised weed of arable land, but both will commonly be found as escapees from cultivation—the white from where it is grown in Cambridgeshire and Essex, and the black from Lincolnshire and Yorkshire.

Mustard Sauce (for eating with grilled herring and mackerel)

Melt 12g ($\frac{1}{2}$oz) butter in a pan, add

2 teaspoons made mustard, 2 teaspoons wine vinegar, $\frac{1}{2}$ teaspoon sugar, salt and black pepper. Mix all together. Finally, add 2–3 tablespoons cream. Serve hot or cold.

Coriander *Coriandrum sativum*

Once ripe, the smell that makes people compare the fruits of coriander to bed-bugs disappears and is replaced by the sweet, orangy odour and soft spicy taste that makes Len Deighton, among others, advise you to 'hurl crushed coriander seeds into every open pot you see.' However, coriander is best employed in cooking stews, pork, sausages, chutneys or pickles. The seeds may also be covered with sugar for a once-popular sweet, coriander comfits.

Oat *Avena fatua*

Oat, 'a grain which in England is generally given to horses, but in Scotland supports the people' ; a remark made by Dr Johnson, who never had a high opinion of the Scots, but which was, up to a certain time, true. Until the introduction of the potato, oats were the staple diet of the Scots. Whisky, bread and porridge were all made from oats. Filleted herrings were dipped in oatmeal before being fried in bacon fat. It was used to thicken soups and oatmeal water was taken to the hayfield to refresh the workers. It was made by putting a handful of oatmeal in a jug, filling the jug up with water and giving it a good stir. Then the grounds were allowed to settle, leaving a liquid more thirst quenching than pure water. Although the wild oat is naturalised and is a pest on arable land, its seed is small in comparison with its cultivated relation. For cooking purposes, permission from a farmer to glean any field he has stripped of its crop will be the most profitable way of obtaining sufficient oats. After threshing, the usual way of preparing the oats was to dry them on the hearth in front of the fire before crushing and bruising them with a pestle and mortar.

Porridge

Sometimes called brose or stirabout. It should be thick enough to support a spoon and is made either with water, with milk or with buttermilk and oatmeal. First bring about 550ml (1pt) of liquid to the boil, and to this add 35g (1$\frac{1}{2}$oz) oatmeal. Sprinkle it in and simmer until cooked. This takes about 20 minutes, but some people like to leave it covered in a low oven overnight. In the morning, more liquid may have to be added if the porridge is looking too thick. Purists eat it plain with just a little salt and, for some reason, while standing up ; others like to add honey, brown sugar and cream.

Oatcakes

Traditionally made only of oatmeal and water, those with less spartan tastes prefer to add some fat.
Mix 450g (1lb) medium ground oatmeal with 4 teaspoons dripping or lard, 1 teaspoon salt and enough warm water to make a dough. Knead until smooth, then dust a board with dry oatmeal, press the dough out on this into a round cake and roll out quite thin. Bake on a hot girdle, cut into triangles. Lift off, rub over lightly with dry meal and toast until crisp before the fire. When ready the oatcakes will curl up.

Herbs

Salad Burnet
Poterium sanguisorba

A cooling cucumber-scented leaf, 'It gives a grace in the drynkynge' declared Gerard, but the young leaves will also add 'grace' to a salad. A limestone-loving plant, it has purple flowers which bloom from June to September, and leaves which Turner, in his *Newe Herball* of 1551, likened to 'the wings of Birdes, standing out as the bird setteth her wings out when she intendeth to flye'.

Wood Sorrel *Oxalis acetosella*

The leaves can be put in salads to take the place of vinegar or lemon dressing. They taste similar, extremely sharp and acid. Wood sorrel's other name is cuckoo's meate from the country belief that the bird cleared its throat by eatings its leaves. A pretty plant, the leaves are clover-shaped and the flowers white. They bloom in April and May.

Thyme *Thymus drucei*

Over forty species of wild thyme have been identified growing in Europe of which three are found in Britain. The only one which is widespread is *T. drucei* common on dry grassland, heaths, dunes and rocky country throughout Britain. It has clusters of pale pink flowers between May and August. Soups, stews, stuffings and sauces all benefit from a sprig of thyme. In the Highlands of Scotland, it was thought that smelling thyme gave one strength and courage and that eating it prevented bad dreams.

Mint *Mentha*

'The smell of Mint does stir up the minde and the taste to a greedy desire of meate'—so said Gerard in the sixteenth century. There are seven kinds of wild mint in Britain, but only four are really suitable for cooking. Of the others, the peppermint is often used as a flavouring for toothpaste and the apple and eau de Cologne mints are dried and put in pot pourris. Corn mint, water mint, horse mint and, the one most often grown in gardens, spearmint, all prefer damp places and are common. They have pinkish flowers blooming generally between July and October. A few leaves chopped and put in cream cheese or sprinkled on top of a tomato salad improve both. Put with new potatoes and peas, or used as a sauce for lamb, mint has no equal.

Marjoram *Origanum vulgare*

Quite common in dry fields on limy soils in the south of England, marjoram has hairy grey-green leaves and bears small pink flowers from July to September. One of the few herbs of which the taste increases when the plant is dried and one of the best herbs for all savoury dishes.

Ramson *Allium ursinum*

Ramson proliferates in woods and shady lanesides. The flowers bloom between April and June. All parts of the plant smell strongly of garlic. The true wild garlic is a different species from ramson and is rare, but ramson, although losing some of its flavour when cooked, makes a good substitute. The chopped stalks can also be used instead of chives.

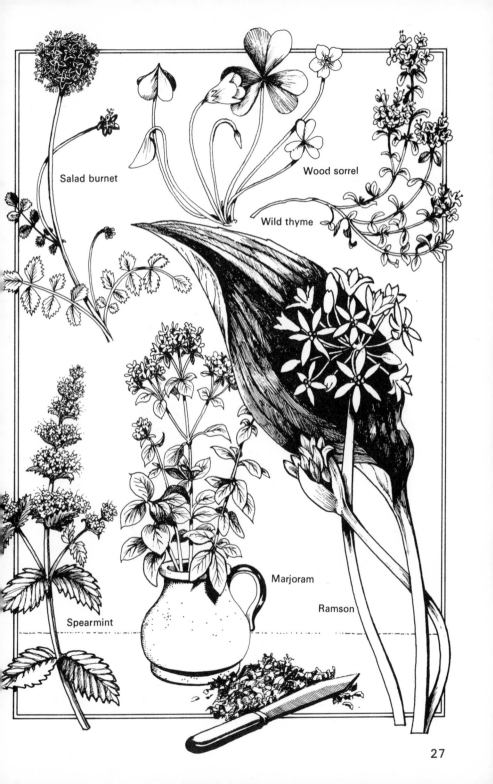

Salad burnet

Wood sorrel

Wild thyme

Marjoram

Ramson

Spearmint

27

Nuts

Walnut *Juglans regia*

The walnut tree, though a native of Persia, was well established in Britain by the sixteenth century. The wood was much used for furniture and the leaves, if gathered in June and July, were used fresh or dried in the treatment of skin diseases or as a dye, recommended by Evelyn 'to colour wooll, woods and hair'. Green walnuts—a valuable source of vitamin C containing even more than rose hips—were used to make a nut liquor. The unripe nuts were beaten down from the trees, a custom which probably gave rise to the old rhyme, 'A dog, a wife and a walnut tree : The more you beat them, the better they be.' Ripe nuts, generally ready by the end of September, should be collected as soon as they begin to fall and spread out in a dry place until the husks fall away. Then, if they are to be stored, clean them well with a brush and water to remove any traces of the husk which otherwise will grow mould. Spread out to dry again and store in airtight earthenware containers, alternating layers of nuts with a mixture of common salt and sand.

Walnut

Walnut Liquor. An Old German Recipe

Chop 450g (1lb) green nuts into small pieces, cover them with 1.4l (2½pt) brandy in a large glass jar. Cover and keep this jar for 2 weeks standing in the sun. Strain the liquid through muslin and pour into a clean jar and add 12g (½oz) pounded cinnamon, 6g (¼oz) pounded cloves and leave the jar again for another week. Boil 300g (12oz) sugar with 625ml (1½pt) water until the sugar falls in large drops from the spoon. Add the nut brandy and strain again.

Walnut Marmalade

Slice 225g (½lb) green walnuts thinly and drop immediately into 550ml (1pt) boiling water to preserve colour. Boil for 40 minutes to soften and reduce walnuts and liquid to 415ml (¾pt). Add 415ml (¾lb) sugar and ¼ teaspoon lemon juice. Boil again until it sets. Makes 450g (1lb) marmalade.

Sweet Chestnut
Castenea sativa

The sweet chestnut was brought to Britain by the Romans. The trees are very long-lived ; there is one in Gloucestershire called the Tortworth Chestnut thought to be the same as one mentioned in 1150 in the deeds of King John and King Stephen. Unfortunately, unless there is a warm spring enabling the tree to flower early and so give the nuts a long enough summer to mature properly, chestnuts do not often ripen in Britain. If they have ripened, they should be collected in October and dried and packed in crocks like walnuts. Chestnuts contain more carbohydrates than other nuts and can be made into all kinds of puddings, bread and stuffings, soup, the famous dessert marron glacé, or best, roasted in the embers of the fire.

Candied Chestnut. American recipe

Shell and peel about 1.1l (2pt) large chestnuts. Cook in boiling water until just tender. Stick with small toothpicks. Heat 2 cups sugar and 1 cup water until it forms a hard ball, add $\frac{1}{4}$ cup rum or maraschino. Dip the chestnuts into the syrup and stand on a cake-rack to cool.

Beechnut *Fagus sylvatica*

The beech only bears nuts every third or fourth year and throughout history the nuts have generally been thought of as food for pigs—the Saxons estimated the worth of a tree by the number of hogs that could 'lie under it'. However, in times of poverty or famine, they have been eaten, roasted and salted, and make good substitutes for almonds. Collect in September and October and roast in an oven until the skin comes off. Then they should be rubbed between two cloths and shaken in a coarse sieve to remove all the hairy down which can cause discomfort if eaten. When quite clean, dry in a cool oven, sprinkle lightly with salt and keep in crocks with well-fitting lids. Beechnut oil is used commercially. 4.5kg (10lb) nuts yield 1.1l (2 pt) oil.

Hazel *Corylus avellana*

The hazel and its cultivated cousin the filbert are the commonest nuts in Britain, found growing as bushes in many hedgerows and as trees in woodlands and in many gardens. Nut walks consisting mainly of hazel and

walnut trees were a popular feature in many gardens ; a good recent example is at Sissinghurst in Kent. Hazelnuts are rich in protein, fat and minerals and are usually ripe and ready for picking by September or October when the husks and shells are quite brown. Squirrels, nuthatches and dormice are all interested in hazels and you may have to race them to get there first. Hazelnuts are best eaten fresh, but also keep well. To store, pick on a dry day, spread on sacking, or in a dry place, turning occasionally until the husks fall off easily. Then store the nuts packed in bran, sand or sawdust in airtight containers. They make good additions to salads and fruit dishes and can be used in making sweets and biscuits.

Baked Apples with Hazelnuts

Scoop out the core of the apples. Mix 25g (1oz) sugar with some ground hazelnuts, a little milk and egg. Stuff apples with this mixture leaving a little heap on the top. Dot with butter, bake slowly in an oven for 30 minutes at 180°C (350°F) gas mark 4. Warm some apple juice and pour over the apples. Bake apples for another 10 minutes and sprinkle with sugar to taste.

Hazel

Grassland Fungi

Field Mushroom
Agaricus campestris

Rule one with all fungi is to identify the species properly before eating. Mistakes are made even with the common field mushroom. People confuse it with the death cap with dire results, although for anyone at all observant this should be impossible. The death cap grows in woodland whereas the field mushroom, as its name presupposes, grows in fields; pastures on which horses have been feeding and have left their droppings are ideal for the field mushroom. They are never surpassed when picked in the early morning, fried in the fat in which the bacon has been cooked and eaten for breakfast. They can also be stewed with parsley and garlic and the small button ones make an excellent champignon à la Greque, but any of the recipes given here are also suitable for field mushrooms.

Champignon à la Greque

Put in a pan 225g ($\frac{1}{4}$pt) water, the juice of $\frac{1}{2}$ lemon, $\frac{1}{2}$ coffee cup (140ml) olive oil, thyme, bayleaf, a piece of celery, black pepper, salt and about 12 coriander seeds, and bring to the boil. Then put in 225g ($\frac{1}{2}$lb) button mushrooms and simmer gently for 5 minutes. Leave to cool in their juice and serve cold with a little of the juice spooned over.

Fairy Ring Champignon
Marasmius oreades

This is the fungi which makes the well known, and to the fervent lawn-keeper dreaded, fairy rings on lawns from June to November. The rings gradually widen and expand as the underground threads, which propagate the fungi, spread outwards. Pale buff in colour, they have a faint smell of sawdust about them and are edible and good. They can be used in all mushroom dishes and, for preserving, dry well. Thread them on a string with knots in between each mushroom and hang in a dry, warm, airy room or spread them out in a cool oven. When thoroughly dry, put them in paper bags and store in a warm place. Before using, soak them in warm water for at least 1 hour and use as you would fresh mushrooms, perhaps for soup.

Mushroom Soup

Finely chop a large onion and cook gently in 50g (2oz) butter until transparent. Coarsely chop 225g ($\frac{1}{2}$lb) mushrooms and add them to the onion and cook for a few minutes. Pour on enough water to come nearly to the top of the vegetables—about 140ml ($\frac{1}{4}$pt). Season well with salt and pepper, cover the pan and cook gently until the vegetables are soft. Put through a blender or vegetable moulé until the mixture is a thick purée. Thin down to required consistency with milk and, if liked, some cream. Check seasoning, reheat and serve.

Parasol and Shaggy Parasol
Lepiota procera and L. rhacodes

The shaggy parasol is squatter and broader and its flavour is not quite as fine as the parasol mushroom. It is also found predominantly in fields, or on roadsides and rubbish tips, while the parasol grows in grassy woodland

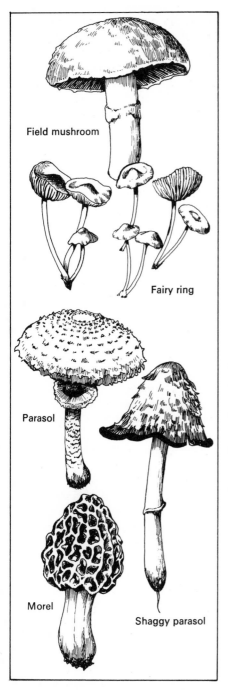

Field mushroom

Fairy ring

Parasol

Shaggy parasol

Morel

clearings. They both have brown, flecked, scaly caps, white gills and a volval ring and appear between August and November. They are huge and one mushroom is almost a meal in itself ; if stuffed, it certainly is.

Stuffed Mushrooms

Melt 1 large chopped onion and a crushed clove of garlic in some fat or butter. Moisten 50g (2oz) breadcrumbs with 2 tablespoons milk and mix with the onion and garlic and 225g ($\frac{1}{2}$lb) good sausagemeat, the chopped stalks of the mushrooms, chopped parsley, salt and pepper and an egg. (Other kinds of meat could be used in place of the sausagemeat such as left over chicken or lamb.) Stuff the mushrooms and bake at 220 °C (425 °F) gas mark 7, for 15–20 minutes.

Morel *Morella esculenta*

There are four edible morel and all of them are spring mushrooms, appearing during March, April and May. Though they vary in size and shape they are instantly recognisable by their brown spongy, honeycomb-like caps. Found in all types of situation with a rich soil, in grassland, hedgerows and gardens. They need to be washed well and blanched in boiling water before cooking. Then they are good used in soups, stews or dried.

Stewed Mushrooms

Stew in butter, meat stock, milk or cream. When soft and cooked, season with salt and pepper, a squeeze of lemon juice and, if liked, some cayenne or paprika pepper.

Bracket Fungi

Beefsteak *Fistulina hepatica*

This fungi gets its name from the texture of the flesh which is thick and fibrous like steak and yields a red juice when cut. It causes a brown rot in the trees on which it grows making the wood, much prized by cabinet makers, a rich brown colour without having any effect on its strength. The fungi is shaped like a hoof with a coarse brown skin and is reasonably common from August to November. Beeksteak has a rather acrid taste like aubergine. It is best to blanch it and cut off the thick rind before cooking, after which it may be sliced and fried with onion and parsley, stewed or made into ketchup.

Mushroom Ketchup

Allow 35g (1½oz) salt to every 450g (1lb) of dry, ripe, broken-up mushrooms. Put in layers with the salt in a stone jar and leave for 3–4 days. Stir and press occasionally. At the end, press well, cover jar and put in a cool oven for 2–3 hours, according to quantity. Strain through a fine sieve pressing gently to extract all the juice and to each 1.1l (1qt) of liquid allow 12g (½oz) allspice, ½ root ginger, 2 blades of mace, 1 chopped shallot and a pinch of cayenne (if liked). Put these in a muslin bag and boil with the liquid for about 2–3 hours or until well reduced. Then, if you have the facilities, put in sterilising bottles and sterilise for 15 minutes. If you haven't, it is not vital but the ketchup may not keep as well. Another improvement is to boil red wine in the proportion of 1 : 4 with the liquid.

Grifola *Grifola frondosa*

Sometimes found at the base of deciduous trees, especially oak, in September and October, a densely tufted, greyish-brown fungi with a rather rancid smell. Poor eating but substantial and may be served as a food in times of need.

Honey Fungus
Armellaria mellea

Another destructive parasite of both frondose and coniferous trees. It grows in clumps at the base of the tree between July and November, is brownish yellow all over, often spotted brown, and has a volval ring. Honey fungus makes good eating, though some find it rather rich. Cook in all the usual ways or use as a stuffing for pigeon, quail or other small birds.

Stuffing

Mince as finely as possible the same weight of parsley and mushrooms. Mince also a little less than half the weight of shallots and cook together in hot butter on a brisk heat for 5 minutes. Season and, if liked, add some breadcrumbs and a beaten egg to the mixture.

Oyster Fungus
Pleurotus ostereatus

A destructive fungus which gradually kills its host tree. It may be found on any frondose tree but is most common on beech and will sometimes attack conifers too. It grows in groups. The shell-like cap is a greyish blue when young, blackening with age ; it has whitish gills and grows the whole year round. When young, it makes good eating. Slice and fry in butter or bake it.

Beefsteak

Grifola

Honey fungus

Oyster fungus

Woodland Fungi

Chanterelle
Cantharellus cibarius

Easily identified and one of the finest edible fungi, chanterelle appear between July and December in deciduous woods. Horn shaped, they are a strong apricot yellow all over and even smell of apricots. Cook them as simply as possible in order not to lose any of their exquisite flavour.

Chanterelle

Slice the chanterelle and cook in butter in a covered frying pan. When tender, add parsley and a tablespoon or so of chicken stock. Stir until the juices are soaked up, then serve.

Cep *Boletus edulis*

Though there are several edible *boletus*, this is the one the gastronomes fancy— known in France as ceps and mentioned as an ingredient in many recipes. Found in leafy woods, especially beech woods, it is large and bulbous with a smooth, brownish cap, spongy white spores instead of gills, a pale brown scaly stalk ; it usually appears from September to November. Cook as field mushrooms but chop the stalk separately as this is tougher than the head. Ceps go well with trout and chicken.

Chicken with Ceps

Flour chicken joints and brown in olive oil, then add 450g (1 lb) sliced ceps.

Cover pan, simmer for 20 minutes, or until chicken is cooked, adding stock from time to time keeping 1 cm ($\frac{1}{2}$in) liquid in the pan. Meanwhile, chop the stalks and mix with 2 chopped cloves of garlic and some chopped parsley, pepper and salt. Transfer the chicken to another dish and keep warm. Put the garlic mixture into the pan and boil fast for 1 minute, pour over chicken and serve.

Wood Mushroom
Agaricus silvicola

Related to the field mushroom, it may be found in all types of woodland between August and November, has a whitish cap, flesh-coloured gills and a loose, volval ring. Cook in the same ways as the field mushroom or make into a purée. It makes an excellent filling for omelettes and is good in sauces for chicken or veal, or as filling for vol au vent cases.

Wood mushroom

Russula

Mushroom Purée

Chop mushrooms finely and cook them slowly in butter—they must not fry. Stew until soft. Season with salt and pepper and a squeeze of lemon, mash and reheat, adding enough bechamel sauce to give the right taste and consistency.

Russula *Russula cyanoxantha*

Another large family easily distinguished by their crisp, white gills, smooth, white stalks and reddish-mauve caps. Several russula are edible but *R. cyanoxantha* is considered the best. This has a pale violet cap which, when peeled, reveals a reddish flesh. It appears between July and

November and may be cooked in all the usual ways. This dish makes a good starter or, on its own, a lunch or supper dish.

Mushrooms on Toast

Heat some butter in a pan and add cleaned, sliced mushrooms. Stew for a few minutes then add parsley or chives, salt and pepper, and about 4 tablespoons cream for 225g ($\frac{1}{2}$lb) mushrooms. Stir for about 5 minutes until it thickens. Serve poured on to toast.

Freshwater Fish

Perch

The perch is a picturesque fish with brightly coloured scales and a large, sharp dorsal fin. It lives in ponds, lakes and slow to moderate-flowing rivers and streams, and lies close to tree roots, large stones and bridges or landing piles. The meat, once the scales and bones are cast aside, is delicious.

Perch

Cook the perch in salted water, made slightly acid with lemon juice. Drain it, skin and put into the court bouillon to make sure that it is quite clean. Drain again, and arrange on a serving dish. Accompany either with a sauce made of melted butter flavoured with lemon juice and chopped parsley or with a hollandaise or bearnaise sauce.

Crayfish

Though strictly crustacean, the crayfish is the edible odd one out, inhabiting fresh rather than salt water— the reason it is included here. Pollution has killed off many of the crayfish which used to inhabit the streams of England. However, they are still to be found in chalk and lime- stone areas of the country. Crayfish are usually caught in baited lobster pots although they can be trapped with a faggot of gorse into which some offal or bad meat is placed—the crayfish crawl in to eat and, one hopes, are unable to crawl out. Madame Prunier claimed that 'there are three kinds of crayfish, or rather three different sizes. The small ones, which average just over an ounce and a half [35g], are used for soups ; the medium sized ones, averaging two ounces [50g], are used for garnishes ; while the larger ones, weighing about three ounces [75g], are used in the recipes which follow.' Before cooking, the crayfish should be washed well, and the intestinal tube removed. This is done with the point of a knife ; the tube is located in an opening under the middle phalanx of the tail. Care should be taken not to break it while pulling it out.

Ecrevisses à la Nage

Make fish stock or court bouillon. Wash the crayfish, drain well and put into the court bouillon. Simmer for 12 minutes. Remove the fish and pile in the middle of a dish and strain the court bouillon over them.

Crayfish

Trout

Not only do trout vie with salmon and

salmon trout (sometimes called sea trout) for the position of the finest fish the gastronome can consume, they are also one of the most sporting fish to catch. For this reason, most rivers stocked with trout are under ownership and permission to fish them is only given at a price. Trout are common in fast-flowing streams, rivers and deep lakes all over Britain. Their prevalence in certain areas is often indicated by the place name. Hence, Troutbeck in the Lake District and Troutsdale in Yorkshire. Trout vary in colour depending on their surroundings and habitat. A fresh trout is never better than when fried in butter or grilled. Ones which have been out of the water some time may benefit from dressing-up.

Trout du Cave

Flour the trout and fry in butter over a moderate heat, allowing 5 minutes a side. Put in a serving dish and keep warm. Cook 75g (3oz) ceps or other mushrooms in the juices in the pan with $\frac{1}{2}$ clove crushed garlic. Season well. Add 2 tablespoons thick cream, salt and pepper. Stir all together, correct the seasoning and pour over the trout. Serve.

Salmon

Salmon fishing is even more highly prized than trout. Gone are the days when housemaids had it written into their contracts that they should not be fed salmon more than a specified number of times a week. Salmon should never be eaten out of season— September to January—as it changes character completely during this time, becoming black and unpalatable.

Migratory, salmon spend the winter in the ocean entering fast-flowing rivers from January onwards returning to their birthplace to spawn.

Salmon

To cook, salmon may be baked or boiled. To bake, wrap in oiled tinfoil with any wine or herbs of your preference and put in a cool oven, 135–150 °C (275–300 °F) gas mark 1–2, allowing 1 hour for a piece or a whole fish up to 2.25kg (5lb) and 12 minutes for every 450g (1lb) after that. To boil a salmon which is to be eaten cold, cover it with cold water, bring to the boil, allow it to simmer for 3 minutes then leave to cool in the water. For a salmon to be eaten hot, put the fish in cold water, bring to the boil and allow 5 minutes' simmering time per 450g (1lb) up to 2.25kg (5lb), 4 minutes for 2.5–3.5kg (6–8lb), and 50–60 minutes in total for 3.5–4.5kg (8–10lb) of fish. Serve with a mayonnaise or hollandaise sauce.

Mayonnaise

2 large egg yolks to 275ml ($\frac{1}{2}$pt) olive oil, 1–2 tablespoons lemon juice or wine vinegar, salt and pepper. Put yolks, salt and pepper in a bowl and whip together. Drip in the olive oil stirring well all the time. As the mayonnaise begins to thicken speed up the rate at which you add the oil. Finally mix in the lemon juice and adjust the seasoning. (If it curdles, break a fresh yolk into a clean bowl and slowly add the curdled mixture to it.)

Freshwater Fish

Bream

Bream likes slow moving, or stagnant water which typically is found in the lowland reaches of large rivers. The French have a proverb that 'he that hath breams in his pond is able to bid his friend welcome.' They are best stuffed or baked in the following manner.

Stuffed Bream

Chop 2–3 slices lean smoked bacon with 1 clove of garlic and a head of fennel. Melt enough oil to cover the base of a frying pan, put in the chopped mixture and cook until the fennel softens. Add about 50–75g (2–3oz) breadcrumbs and a beaten egg. Stuff the fish with this, then grill, basting with some rosemary and lemon juice.

Baked Bream

Lay chopped shallots and breadcrumbs in the bottom of an oven dish and place the bream on top. Cover with more shallots and breadcrumbs, pour on some white wine and dot with butter. Bake for 25 minutes.

Carp

A still-water fish, it will survive in conditions where others would die for lack of oxygen. For this reason, from the Middle Ages to the present day, the carp has been popular for domestic fish ponds and for fish farming. Carp are very long-lived and grow to 22kg (50lb) in weight. It was once thought that by eating carp some of their longevity was passed on to the consumer. Carp are inclined to be muddy and should be soaked in

vinegar and water (6 tablespoons to 2.2l [4pt] water) for a few hours after cleaning and before cooking. The bitter gall sack at the back of the neck should be removed and some cooks like to take off the scales as well. This is facilitated by dipping the fish for a minute in boiling water. Tench is a relative of the carp and may be cooked in the same ways.

Mourette de Carpe

Simmer together 100g (4oz) sliced mushrooms, 1 medium onion chopped, 75g (3oz) currants, 3 large cloves garlic, a bouquet garni and 1 bottle red Burgundy for $\frac{1}{2}$ hour in an uncovered pan until the wine has reduced by one third. Season. Cut the cleaned carp into pieces. Add to the pan, cover and simmer for another $\frac{1}{2}$ hour or until the fish is cooked. Mash together 50g (2oz) butter, 1 tablespoon flour and use it to thicken the sauce. Serve hot.

Pike

Pike lie concealed in weeds or holes until a smaller fish passes close enough to be grabbed and eaten. They can then move at incredible speed. Weedy rivers, streams and ponds all over Britain will be likely to have their supply of pike. The flesh, inclined to be dry to the taste, is improved by being left in salt for 12 hours before cooking. It can then be cut in steaks coated with egg and breadcrumbs and fried and served with a horse-radish sauce (see p 12). Pike are also good stewed.

Stewed Pike

Clean and scale the pike discarding the roe with the rest of the innards. Chop together 6 shallots, 1 onion and some parsley. Butter an oven dish and lay the vegetables in the bottom and place the pike on top. Sprinkle with lemon juice, salt and pepper, and pour on enough stock and white wine, half and half, to cover it. Bake in a fairly hot oven, 190 °C (375 °F) gas mark 5, for about 30 minutes or until cooked.

Eel

Eels breed in the ocean, migrating to rivers when about 7cm (3in) long. Called elvers at this stage, they are caught in great numbers, especially at the mouth of the Severn river, washed in salt water and fried like whitebait. The elvers that manage to bypass the elver nets spend the next seven to twelve years in the river before migrating back to the ocean. As they migrate down river in autumn, traps are laid to catch them. At other times eels can be netted and speared, using a long three-pronged fork which is jabbed down into the mud where the eels lie. Once caught, an eel is a wriggly thing to kill, and even after death it is helpful to place the eel on newspaper to stop it moving. Correctly, the spinal cord should be pierced by a skewer at the back of the neck but the uninitiated might find it easier to chop off the head. Skin the eel by making an incision round its neck and pulling the skin backwards from the top, rather like taking off a stocking. Eels may be cut in sections and smoked, or floured and fried, or stewed. Here is a recipe derived from one of Madame Prunier's:

Anguille à la Romanaise

Cut the eel in pieces 5cm (2in) long, and wrap each piece up in a very thin slice of raw lemon without the rind and a thin rasher of streaky bacon. Tie up, and cook gently in butter, in a stewpan, adding 2 cloves of garlic. As soon as they are cooked, take out the pieces, untie them, and arrange them on a dish. Remove the garlic, swill the stewpan with a glass of dry white wine, let it reduce, and thicken it with butter. Cover the pieces of eel with it, and sprinkle them with chopped parsley.

(*above*) Bream   (*below*) Carp

Seawater Fish

Dab

A member of the plaice family, dab is a flat fish inhabiting inshore waters all around Britain in summer but is most frequently found off sandy banks at 20–24m (11–12 fathoms). Dabs may be caught with a rod and line. Fresh dabs should be plain grilled, or covered with egg and breadcrumbs and fried. Dabs which have been out of the water for a little while will be improved by dressing-up.

Marinaded Dab

Remove head, fins and tail. Wipe fish. Make a vinaigrette dressing from 2 parts oil to 1 part wine vinegar or lemon juice, 1 sliced onion, 1 chopped clove of garlic, 1 bayleaf, 1 teaspoon chopped chives, salt and pepper. Pour into a dish and lay the dabs on top. Leave for 2 hours turning frequently. After draining, grill, basting with the strained marinade mixture. Serve with parsley butter.

Whiting

They inhabit shallow, sandy bottomed waters and are common everywhere but particularly in the North Sea. They take a bait and can be caught with rod and line. A member of the cod family, whiting have the characteristic firm, white, flaky flesh and can be used for all the same recipes. Most whiting are filleted before cooking, the blunt head cut off and the backbone removed from the back, rather than the front, as you would a kipper. Cover with egg and breadcrumbs and fry or cook in a sauce. This is a Normany recipe quoted by Jane Grigson in *Fish Cookery*:

Les Filets de Merlian Vallée d'Auge

'Cook 10oz [250g] chopped onion gently in 5 tablespoons oil until soft and golden. Season and put in a large gratin dish. Lay 6 boned whiting on top and season well. Pour ½pt [275ml] dry cider over them and sprinkle 2oz [50g] grated gruyère cheese on top. Cook in an oven [gas mark 4–5] [180–190 °C, 350–375 °F] for about 20 minutes or until the fish are cooked.'

Flounder

A flat fish, in summer it can be found in estuaries and inshore waters flapping along the bottom of the seabed. Flounder live on molluscs, especially cockles, and take a bait freely. 'The flounder is in taste, digestion and nourishment, like unto the plaice, especially if he be young', to quote Venner's *Via recta ad vitam longam*, Ed 1628, but most people would not rate it as high as this. Prepare for cooking by removing the head, cutting off side fins and tail.

Flounder au Gratin

Wipe prepared fish well. Chop together parsley, chervil, 1–2 shallots, onion or chives and a few mushrooms. Butter an oven dish and put $\frac{2}{3}$ of the herb mixture in the bottom, add $\frac{1}{2}$ cup water or fish stock and $\frac{1}{2}$ cup white wine, salt and pepper. Then place in the fish and sprinkle the remaining $\frac{1}{3}$ of the herbs on top with a covering of brown breadcrumbs. Dot with butter, add a little lemon juice and cook in a moderate oven for 20–30 minutes, basting occasionally. Brown surface under grill if required and serve.

Mackerel

Migrating to deeper water in winter, in summer mackerel are spasmodically abundant in shoals all around the coast of Britain, although stocks are now diminishing. They are caught with a rod and line or in nets. Mackerel quickly deteriorate and should be eaten very fresh. An oily fish, small ones are best grilled. Make a couple of incisions in the back first and serve with a sorrel or gooseberry sauce. Larger ones should be baked.

Gooseberry Sauce

Top and tail 450g (1lb) gooseberries, put in a pan and cover with water. Bring to the boil and simmer until soft but not falling apart. Drain. Make a white sauce with 25g (1oz) butter, 25g (1oz) flour and 415ml ($\frac{3}{4}$pt) milk. Mix in the gooseberries and a dessertspoon chopped fennel leaves and season with salt and pepper, nutmeg and lemon juice and, if needed some sugar.

Baked Mackerel

Make a sauce by cooking a large, chopped onion gently in 2 tablespoons oil, then stir in 1 tablespoon flour and 225ml (8oz) dry white wine and 225ml (8oz) water. Add a bouquet garni and, when the sauce is smooth and moderately thick, 2 heaped tablespoons French mustard and seasoning. Pour it over some cleaned mackerel placed head to tail in a buttered dish and bake in a fairly hot oven, 205 °C (400 °F) gas mark 6, for 20 minutes or until the fish is cooked.

Cod

Most of the cod found in fishmongers are caught in northern waters round Iceland, where the fish migrate for the winter. However, in summer they are to be found in shoals in shallower water, 30–80m (16–44 fathoms), around the coast of Britain, where they feed on worms and small fish. Cod are really best covered with egg and breadcrumbs and fried and served with a parsley, hollandaise or bearnaise sauce.

Molluscs

Mussel *Mytilus edulis*

From the mid tide-line down, on all types of shore where there are rocks or stones for attachment, mussels will be abundant and are one of the most delicious molluscs. A Mr King taking part in Darwin's voyage on HMS *Beagle* described how the natives of Chile cooked mussels in the ground. They first dug a hole, then lined the bottom with smooth stones on which they lit a fire. When the stones were sufficiently hot, the ashes were cleared away, the mussels heaped on the stones and covered first with leaves and straw and then earth. They cooked in their own juice.

Moules Marinières

Scrape and brush the shells of the mussels until clean. For 2l (3½pt) mussels put in a pan 1 chopped medium-sized onion, 1 finely chopped shallot, some parsley stalks, thyme, bayleaf, freshly ground pepper and 8 tablespoons white wine. Add the mussels and cover tightly. Cook over a fast heat and at the end of 2 minutes shake the mussels. Do this 2–3 times more and at the end of 6 minutes the mussels should be cooked. Remove the top shell from each mussel and arrange them in a deep, heated dish and keep warm. Boil up the remaining liquor, add some butter and chopped parsley, and strain over the mussels.

There are endless variations on this theme. Some add garlic to the mixture and others add some spoonfuls of hollandaise sauce to the strained mussel liquor instead of butter and then reheat without boiling. Still another variation is to cover them with a cheese sauce made with the liquor to which chives have been added ; the dish is then browned under the grill just before serving.

Shrimp *Crangon vulgaris*

Widely distributed and locally abundant, shrimps are found on sandy shores at the lower end of the tide-line in pools and river estuaries. Specially constructed shrimp nets are used to catch them, pushed along the sandy bottom near rocks in low water. The stealthy manage to catch them in rock pools with the aid of a butterfly-type shrimping net. Others bait a fine meshed lobster pot with a piece of fish or entrail and leave it in a strategic place. And yet another way is to bait a netted hoop, drop it to the sea bottom on a rope, leave it for a while and, when it is pulled up, pray that it is full of shrimps. The best way of eating shrimps is to boil them in salted water for 3–5 minutes and then, pulling off the shells, eat them plain or with a little mayonnaise. Small ones are good potted and it is also a successful way of preserving them.

Potted Shrimps

'Melt 3 or 4oz [75–100g] butter in a saucepan, and into it cast a pint [550ml] of picked shrimps, a blade of mace powdered, cayenne and, if liked, some grated nutmeg. Heat them up slowly, but do not let them boil. Pour them into little pots, and when they are cold, cover with melted butter. One experiment will tell you just how much pepper and spice to use.' *Pottery*, A. Potter, Wine and Food Society, 1946.

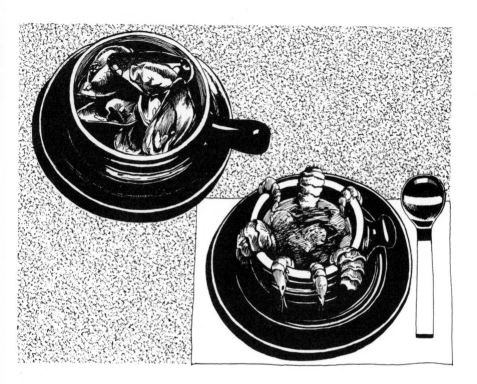

Lobster *Homarus vulgaris*

Lobsters are in season from April or May until October. They were common and cheap but overfishing has made them rare and very expensive. They are generally caught in baited lobster pots attached to ropes which are lowered down on to the seabed where the shore rocks end and the sand begins. A surer way of getting a lobster is to exchange money with a local lobster fisherman— every west-coast seaside village seems to have one. They will be totally fresh and cheaper than any you can buy in a shop. To cook, put the live lobster in a pan and cover with cold water and a firm lid. Bring it slowly to the boil. The gradual heating of the water anaesthetises the lobster and it feels no pain. Allow 15 minutes simmering time for the first 450kg (1 lb) lobster and 10 minutes for each subsequent one. Once cooked, remove from the water and allow to cool. The fine taste of lobster should not be obscured by rich sauces—a little home-made mayonnaise is all that is required as accompaniment.

Crab *Cancer pagurus*

Found from the middle to lower tide-line in rocks, seaweed and under stones, crabs are caught with a baited lobster pot ; they are much more common and easy to find. Cook in the same way as lobster, allow to cool and then remove all the meat from shell and legs. Dress with a vinaigrette or mayonnaise dressing and serve heaped up in the shell.

Molluscs

Whelk *Nucella lapillus*

A type of marine snail with a horny shell. The whelk is commonly found on rocks often in association with mussels. They used to be specially abundant on the Cheshire coast and were sold in quantities in Liverpool. Clean, soak and boil for 5 minutes. After this they are good made into soup or steamed for 1 hour and served in a parsley sauce.

Oyster *Osterea edulis*

It is unlikely today that you will find many uncultivated oysters. Overfishing and pollution have diminished the numbers that used to inhabit the estuarine waters of England. Any that still exist lie in carefully tended beds mostly around the east coast, Whitstable, Colchester and Orford and there are still some uncultivated oysters off the Scottish coast. British oysters are considered the finest in the world. Purists eat them raw, the shell prised open at its hinge with a knife, then perhaps sprinkled with a little lemon juice and swallowed whole. But in the days when Sam Weller could remark that 'poverty and oysters always seem to go together' raw oysters were reserved for invalids. The wealthy, if they ate them at all, cooked them in various ways. They were dipped in egg and breadcrumbs and fried, stuffed into steaks which were then grilled, included in steak pies, wrapped in thin rashers of bacon, put on skewers, grilled and served on toast, or stewed. But however they were cooked, care was taken not to overcook them as this made them tough. Madame Prunier lists twenty-nine recipes for oysters in her book of fish cookery. This is taken from one of them:

Devilled Oysters

Poach several dozen oysters in their own liquor, drain them, and remove their beards. With the oyster liquor

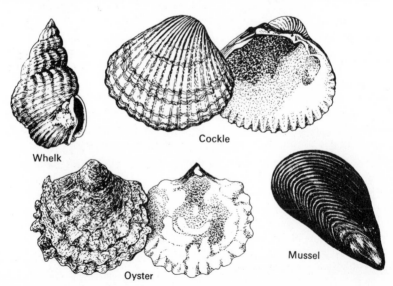

Whelk

Cockle

Oyster

Mussel

and some fresh cream make a bechamel sauce ; season it with salt, grated nutmeg and a pinch of paprika pepper. Mix the oysters with this sauce, and garnish the concave shells with the mixture. Sprinkle with fried breadcrumbs, arrange the shells on a baking sheet, and put them in the oven for a few minutes before serving them. Be careful not to let them boil.

Cockle *Cardium edule*

Abundant in certain areas where there are sandy, muddy shores, cockles live below the middle to lower shore-line. As the tide recedes, cockles tend to burrow down quickly about 5–7cm (2–3in) into the sand. Cockle-gatherers rake them up using a blunt rake, going carefully in order not to break their shells and taking only those measuring more than 2.5cm (1in) across. To prepare, wash the shells and stand in fresh water for 6 hours, then plunge in boiling water for 5 minutes. Eat by removing the meat from the shells. Serve them plain in a vinaigrette dressing or add them to mixed seafood salads or make them into cockle pie.

Cockle Pie

Butter a deep pie-dish. Boil the cockles, remove the meat and put in a little milk. Strain the liquor in which they were boiled and use to make a white sauce with butter, flour, a spoonful of anchovy essence and a shake of nutmeg. Sprinkle brown breadcrumbs into the pie-dish, cover with dabs of butter, then put in a layer of cockles. Pour over some of the white sauce, and add another layer of crumbs, butter and cockles. Continue in this way until the dish is full. Cover with a layer of mashed potato and bake for 30 minutes. Serve with slices of lemon.

Limpet *Pattela vulgata*

Their conical shells will be seen on most rocky shores clinging to the rocks with the aid of a powerful sucker. They are said to produce a resistance of 67kg (150lb). Prise them off the rock with a knife and wash them. Then soak them in water for several hours and boil for 5 minutes. Remove from the shells and simmer for a further 30 minutes. Limpets are sometimes called the Poor Man's Oyster and can be used instead of mussels or oysters in any recipe, but they are always somewhat rubbery to eat.

Periwinkle *Littorina littorea*

Found clinging to rocks and weeds on the shore-line between high and low tides, periwinkle are very common. A large family, of which the common periwinkle is the biggest, and therefore the one most worth eating. Before cooking, they should be soaked overnight in clean water in a carefully covered container—they are great escapers. Then plunge them in boiling, salted water and simmer for 10 minutes. To eat, heap a pile on your plate and 'winkle' out the tiny bodies with a pin, discarding the black head at the base of each shell. Some people like to dip them in pepper and vinegar.

Seaweed

Sea Lettuce *Ulva lactuca*

Sea lettuce is broad, flat, irregular-shaped, membraneous and translucent seaweed up to 46cm (18in) long. Watery green in colour, it grows in bunches and is common on most rocky shores during July and August. Similar to laver, it may be cooked and served in all the same ways although the results are less good. It was thought to cure scrofula for which it was eaten during the eighteenth century in England. It was also sold in the markets of Peking and Canton as a fever-reducing medicine.

Laver *Porphyra umbilicalis*

A large, lobed, irregular-shaped, thin and membraneous seaweed, in colour laver is a dark, purplish red becoming almost black when dry and greenish brown when old. Widely distributed, it grows on rocks and stones at all levels on exposed beaches, especially where the rocks are covered with sand. On these the weed appears to be growing in the sand. There are two other species of *Porphyra* with which *P. umbilicalis* may be confused but since they are all edible and can be cooked in the same way, this will not matter. Laver, which is rich in iodine, is at its best between late autumn and spring and is the seaweed most commonly eaten in Britain. Even today, laver cakes are often eaten for breakfast in Wales. It may also be served as an accompaniment to roast mutton. Potted laver used to be sold at Fortnum and Mason and was eaten for health reasons in eighteenth-century Bath. Laver is prepared by first steeping it in water for 3–4 hours, then boiling it until tender. After this the water should be strained off and the laver beaten to a pulp. This can be made into soup, dressed with oil and vinegar for salad, reheated with salt, pepper, butter and cream for a vegetable or

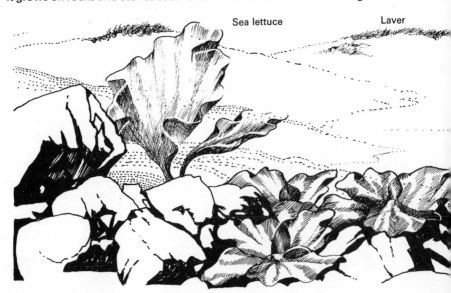

Sea lettuce   Laver

made into laver cakes and served with bacon for breakfast.

Laver Cakes

Take some boiled laver and dress it with butter and cream and season well. Mix in enough oatmeal to enable you to form it into cakes the size of small fishcakes. Toss in oatmeal and fry in bacon fat.

Carragheen *Chrondus crispus*

Changeable in appearance, carragheen varies from having a stalk of 15cm (6in) to almost none at all, from having a wide, flat and much divided frond to being narrow and scarcely branched, and from being a dark red to being green when exposed to a lot of sun. It is found in abundance on all types of shore and is widely distributed. Commercially, carragheen is used as a basis for ice-cream, pastries, cough mixtures and toothpaste. In 1919 a record harvest of 2,000 wet tons was taken from the coast of Brittany for these purposes. Carragheen is eaten by local populations on the east coast of the USA and Canada, on the west coast of Europe and in Ireland—usually in the form of a mould. The seaweed is collected, washed, laid out in the sun, and sprinkled occasionally with salt water until it is dry. Then it can be kept until required or used fresh. Very poor people used to boil carragheen in water which was then strained and left to set. The resulting jelly was eaten cold. However, it is more appetising if some flavouring is added.

Carragheen Mould

Soak $\frac{1}{2}$ cup dried carragheen in water for 10 minutes, drain it, simmer for 15 minutes in milk with a flavouring of elder flowers (2 teaspoons), nutmeg or sweet spice. Strain it into a basin or mould, sweeten with honey or sugar and leave to set.
A fruit jelly may be made by using water instead of milk and adding the juice of stewed fruit.

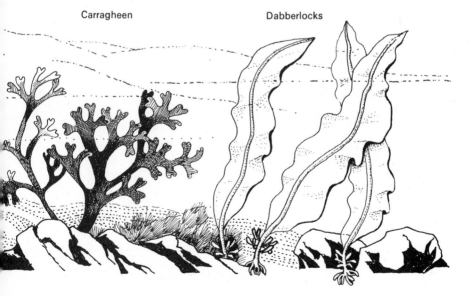

Carragheen   Dabberlocks

Seaweed

Sweet Tangle
Laminaria saccharina

Browny-yellow, sweet tangle has flat fronds from 20–243cm (8in–8ft) in length and up to 30cm (1ft) wide, and attaches itself to small stones and rocks from the middle shore downwards. Sweet tangle is one of the most prolific seaweeds, found on almost any kind of shore, but particularly sandy ones with rock pools. It is known as the Poor Man's Weather Glass owing to the fact that a frond hung up will become soft and limp at the approach of rain, and dry and brittle in fine spells. The whole frond is also coated with a whitish efflorescence which is sweet to the taste, hence its scientific name of *saccharina* and its common name of sugar wrack—although it bears no relation to the wrack, *Fucacia* family. Both horses and humans are said to enjoy sugar wrack. There is evidence that the young stalks with their sweet, peanuttish flavour were eaten throughout Europe. According to Greville, writing in 1830, it used to be sold by fishermen in the streets of Edinburgh to the cry of 'Buy dulse and tangle' and according to V. J. Chapman in *Seaweeds and their Uses*, a seaweed bread of sweet tangle and carragheen called 'Pain des Algues' used to be made on the coast of America. It took the form of a jelly. In Norway during World War II the Germans erected two bakeries to make bread from the desalinated algae.

The Japanese make a substance called kan-hoa which they add to soups, vegetables and boiled rice. The weed is washed, hung out until almost dry, then rolled up and put in presses to dry further. Finally it is shredded with a sharp knife and laid out in the open until the surface is dry but still contains enough moisture to keep it pliable for at least a year. The Commander Islanders in the Behring Sea eat *L. Bongardina*, a relative of sweet tangle. First it is cooked, then minced, mixed with pepper, salt, onion, tomatoes and flour, and finally fried.

Dulse *Rhodymenia palmata*

Variable in shape and size, from 10–35cm (4–14in), dulse resembles an irregular-shaped hand for its small pieces grow like fingers from a broad, central palm. Dark red in colour with purple overtones, it is found on the middle to lower shore growing from an anchoring disc which may be attached to rocks or other seaweeds such as *Fucus* and *Laminaria*. Widely distributed on all types of beach, its age may be ascertained by the size of the holdfast disc, which increases in thickness each year. For eating, the younger the seaweed the better the taste, but even then it is likely to be tough and the flavour salty. Popularly known as dulse in England and Scotland, *dillesk* in Ireland and *sol* in Iceland where it was a regular item of commerce which was traded between the inhabitants of the coast and the people of the interior between the twelfth and nineteenth centuries. It has been eaten in various ways ; washed, dried and made into small rolls to be used as a 'chew' like tobacco or chewing-gum ; uncooked as a salad ; boiled in milk or oil of citron—a dish some have pronounced delicious ; and

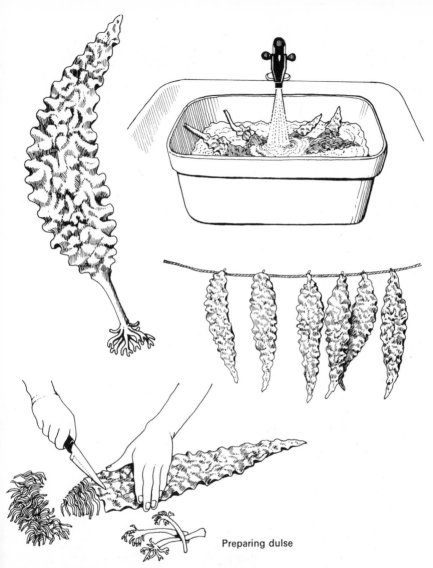

Preparing dulse

cooked as a vegetable to be eaten with dried fish, butter and potatoes. It has also been used as a flavouring for soups, and, in times of famine, has been baked into bread. It is also an essential part of the diet of certain sheep, notably North Ronaldsay, a breed indigenous to the Orkneys. In Norway dulse is called *son-söll* or sheep's weed.

Stewed Dulse. Irish country recipe from Portaferry
Wash freshly gathered dulse to remove the sand and grit. Put it in a saucepan with milk, butter, salt and pepper and stew until tender. This can take from 3–4 hours. Use it as a supper dish with oatcakes or brown bread.

49

Water Birds

Gull

All gulls are edible and in former times were much esteemed, very expensive and thought a delicacy. Frequently they were caught and specially fattened for the pot. They would be taken when young from their nests, put into large barns and fed on, among other things, dogs' flesh. Gulls which have fed exclusively on fish do tend to taste very fishy. Skinned, then casseroled or roasted and served with a mustard and vinegar sauce (see p 24) they used to feature on West-Country hotel menus.

Coot or Moorhen

Coots and moorhens are often confused with each other, both being small, black birds inhabiting freshwater ponds and streams. However, they can be identified as the coot has a yellow bill with a white mark above it, while the moorhen has a red beak without a white mark. In former times, the coot was eaten more frequently and was sold in markets, appearing, often disguised under a more glamorous name, on the menus of London restaurants. Both birds are protected during their breeding season. They should be skinned before cooking but even then are inclined to be tough. Casserole with vegetables.

Duck

All duck are protected during their breeding season and all are edible. However, they do vary in flavour and according to which time of year they are killed. A duck's meat will taste of the food on which it has eaten. If this is fish, the flavour can be overpowering and the bird may need soaking. However, when taken from inland waters where they feed on molluscs and plants, mallard, pochard, shoveller, teal and wigeon are all fairly common and have well-flavoured flesh. Less fat and more like game than the domestic duck, they are best roasted or cooked with something sweet.

Wild Duck with Black Cherries

'For 6 people take 3 duck and put in a roasting dish with enough chicken stock and wine to cover the bottom. Sprinkle the birds generously with

Coot

emon rind and about 100g (4oz) butter. Place in a hot oven 220–230 °C (425–450 °F) gas mark 7–8, for 15 minutes, then turn on their sides and cook for a further 15 minutes. Repeat this process twice more. Add the segments of 4 oranges peeled and skinned, and a large tin of black cherries. Turn the duck right side up and cook for another 15 minutes. Reduce the heat to 170–190 °C (325–375 °F) gas mark 3–5 and leave for about another 20 minutes. If the breasts are still not cooked, increase the heat for a further 10 minutes. Minimum total cooking time : 1½ hours.' Suki Kinloch.

Goose

Wild geese come under schedule 3 in the Birds Protection Act, that is 'Wild birds which may be killed or taken outside the close season', are the bean, canada, greylag, pink foot and whitefront. The greylag, a pale grey goose with an orangy yellow beak and pink feet, is the most common in Britain and large flocks may be seen in winter in estuaries and on arable land especially in Scotland. To eat, wild geese are quite different from domestic geese, much gamier in flavour and the flesh darker and drier. Formerly, in the north of Scotland, smoked goose formed part of the breakfast menu. Most old recipes recommend some preliminary salting before cooking, which usually took the form of boiling with spices and garlic. Today wild goose is generally roasted, but in order to prevent it from becoming too dry, the bird is first wrapped in a coat of bacon at then cooked in a hot oven making sure not to overcook. A sweet sauce is generally served as an accompaniment.

Fruit Sauce for Game

'1lb [450g] red plums or damsons, ½lb [225g] sugar, 1in [2.5cm] cinnamon stick, 2 cloves, 2 tablespoons redcurrant jelly, 1 glass port wine, 1½oz [35g] butter.
Choose ripe plums and wash or wipe them carefully. Put them into a lined or earthenware saucepan with the sugar, cloves, and cinnamon, but without any water, and stew them slowly until reduced to a pulp. Then rub the fruit through a fine sieve and return the purée to a clean saucepan. Add the redcurrant jelly and port wine, bring to the boil and simmer for a few minutes. Then draw the saucepan to the side of the fire and add the butter in small pieces. Do not boil again after the butter is added. The sauce may be used either hot or cold'. *Cookery for Every Household*, Florence B. Jack, 1931.

Salted Goose

'A goose, 2oz [50g] saltpetre, 7oz [200g] sugar, 3lb [1.3kg] salt.
Boil up 5 quarts [5.5l] of water with the saltpetre, sugar and salt, and pour hot over the goose, which has been cleaned and trussed. Leave the goose lying in this decoction for three days, then boil slowly until tender. The goose should be served cold with a horse-radish sauce.' *The Tenth Muse*, Sir Harry Luke, 1954.

Land Birds

Pigeon

Fat from the farmer's corn, pigeons of all varieties are delicious to eat. However, I cannot say how good those are, fat from tourists' bread and London dustbins. Pigeons breed prolifically and are considered a menace by those who have to deal with them. Anyone who removes some from circulation for the pot will be performing a service. Young ones, their breasts covered with bacon and brushed with butter, can be roasted. Old ones are inclined to be very tough and should be casseroled. People who have a glut of pigeons often just take off the breast and cook this, discarding the rest or making it into soup. Here is a translation of an Escoffier recipe by Elizabeth David :

Stewed Pigeons

'Two or three young pigeons, dressed and drawn but not trussed, are to be lightly browned in butter and transferred to a terrine or other small pot. Into the butter in which the pigeons have been browned, pour a little glass of cognac and one of white wine ; let this boil a few seconds and pour it over the pigeons. Surround the birds with a few little onions and mushrooms, also previously cooked in butter. Season with salt and pepper, add a few spoonfuls of good veal stock, cover the pigeons with little pieces of lean bacon first cooked in butter until the fat has run ; seal the pot hermetically and cook in a gentle oven for 50 minutes [longer for older pigeons]'.

Rook

Rooks inhabit agricultural areas, nesting in colonies in tree tops all over the British Isles. There is a country saying that if the rooks build their nests high in the trees a good summer will follow. A fully-grown rook is rank and unfit to eat but, in country areas, the breast and thigh tops of young rooks were often stewed or put in a pie.

Sparrow

The idea of eating the garden sparrow does seem quite unlikely. No matter how often he takes the top off your growing plants, he is nevertheless a chirpy fellow and one that you would be loath to catch and put in the pot. However, in former times he was eaten frequently in rural areas both in the UK and on the continent, either plucked, drawn and put in a pie or pushed on to a skewer and grilled. Only the breasts were eaten.

Sparrow Pie

Pluck and draw the birds and stuff them with some veal forcemeat. Line the bottom and sides of a pie-dish with thin slices of steak. Put in the birds, cut in halves. Season with salt and pepper and intersperse with sections or slices of hardboiled eggs. Half-fill the dish with stock, cover with shortcrust pastry and bake in a moderately hot oven for about $1\frac{1}{2}$ hours, depending on the size.

Game-Bird

All birds that come under this heading are protected during their breeding season. They are usually closely watched at other times, too, great care having been taken by the owner of the

(from left to right)
grouse, partridge, pheasant

porting rights to preserve their
habitat and to encourage their
proliferation. Under the game-bird
category come pheasants and
woodcock, which live in woodland,
partridge found on pastureland, snipe
in boggy and marshy areas, and grouse
found on moorland. If a game-bird
comes your way by design or accident
–pheasants are often run over by
passing cars—the best way of cooking
will be to roast or, if of uncertain age,
casserole it, following the recipe for
stewed pigeons (see above). Hanging
improves the taste of all birds ; hang
pheasant for 3-12 days, partridge for
3–4 days and grouse for 4–7 days.

Roast Bird

Small birds such as snipe and
woodcock should only be plucked—
not drawn—and cooked with their
innards in. Larger birds, after plucking,
should have their heads, feet and
innards removed. Stand the bird on a
piece of toast to catch the juice while
it is cooking, cover the breast with
bacon, dot with butter and roast in a
fairly hot oven. 20 minutes is enough
for snipe, about 40 minutes for grouse,
and 1 hour for pheasant. Serve on the
toast with a gravy made from the
juices in the pan. The traditional
accompaniments for pheasant are
bread sauce and fried breadcrumbs.

Animals

Deer

Of the three common species of deer in Great Britain, gastronomically the roe deer is considered the finest, followed by the fallow deer and then the red deer. Fallow deer inhabit lowland deciduous woods mainly in England and Ireland. Roe deer are common in Scotland, and in parts of northern and southern England, in scrubland and open woods. Red deer live in mountainous areas in Scotland and England.

However, their flesh falls under the overall title of venison and they are all cooked in the same way. Deer should only be taken outside their breeding season and usually belong to the person on whose land they are roaming. Although some culling of deer is necessary, there is much indiscriminate poaching which, if uncontrolled, could lead to their total destruction. Deer are at their best under three years old ; after this age the meat becomes tough. Before cooking, all venison should be hung for 12–21 days in a cool, airy place. The meat is inclined to be dry and should be liberally larded or wrapped in bacon fat and roasted slowly. Rowan jelly is a traditional accompaniment (see p 22).

Venison in Red Wine

Tie a shoulder or flank of venison in a sausage and put to marinade for 24 hours in 8 tablespoons red wine and 1 tablespoon olive oil. Remove meat, wipe it dry and roll in flour. Pack tightly in an oval dish and cover with a layer of sliced onions and one of bacon fat. Pour over the marinade, season with salt and pepper, cover closely and cook at electricity 115 °C (310 °F) gas mark 2 for 4–4½ hours. Serve with redcurrant or rowan jelly.

Hare

In England the common brown hare is found on all kinds of open, rough ground. In Ireland it is rare, its place being taken by the Arctic or blue hare. Both hide up during the day in 'forms', nests which they make in dense vegetation, and emerge at night to feed. Both are edible and delicious. Young hares have a flesh almost like chicken and should be cooked by roasting. Older animals should be hung for a week and then are best marinated and made into the classic dish of jugged hare.

Jugged Hare

Put a jointed hare in a large bowl and pour over 1 glass of wine vinegar, ½ glass olive oil, salt and pepper, a bunch of thyme and a sliced onion. Leave for 12 hours turning at intervals. Chop an onion and put with 25g (1oz) pork fat and 50g (2oz) butter in a pan. Add the pieces of hare and cook together for about 20 minutes, turning occasionally. Sprinkle with flour and add the marinade mixture, 275ml (½pt) beef stock and enough red wine to cover. Allow to simmer for 1½ hours. Optional additions are a glass of port and a glass of the hare's blood.

Rabbit

Doe rabbits taste better than buck rabbits which, especially if in season, can be very strong-tasting. As with all

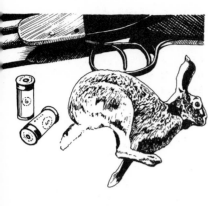

Lapin Chasseur

Joint a rabbit and sauté pieces in 25g (1oz) butter and 75g (3oz) diced pork until brown, together with some small shallots or chopped onions. Add some thyme, bayleaf and about $1\frac{1}{2}$ glasses white wine. Simmer for about 1 hour until tender. Add about 100g (4oz) mushrooms which have been fried in a little butter. Finally, mix in 1 small cup cream and/or the yolk of an egg. Sprinkle with chopped parsley and serve.

Rabbit Stew

Joint a rabbit and soak for 12 hours in a marinade of 1 part vinegar, 2 parts cider, some bay leaves, thyme, rosemary, fennel, salt and pepper. Drain the rabbit, dry, smother with butter and onion and brown. Place in a casserole with 100g ($\frac{1}{4}$lb) sliced, dried apricots (which have been soaked previously). Add 2 tablespoons flour to the butter in which the rabbit has been fried and mix with a little water, then pour over the rabbit with the marinade and more water or stock if required. Simmer until tender and before serving add 1 tablespoon redcurrant jelly if liked.

animals, the younger the rabbit the more tender the flesh. You can tell if a rabbit is young by its fragile jaw and easily-torn ears. Rabbits were introduced into this country in the twelfth century by the Normans both for food and sport. Rather surprisingly, it took them until the nineteenth century to reach and colonise Scotland. Their prolific numbers were temporarily reduced by myxomatosis, but now a new and largely immune species has developed and in most areas they are back to their original strength. Rabbits are great breeders and eat almost all kinds of vegetation—up to 180kg (400lb) of fresh food per year. They live in warrens, which may be found on grassland, woodland, arable land, sand-dunes, marshes, moorlands and cliffs. Rabbits can be caught with ferrets or dogs, and are easily netted or shot, especially at night when they are dazzled by the headlights of a car. After skinning, tender young rabbits can be simply jointed, brushed with butter and grilled or fried. Older ones are better stewed. Use the recipe for jugged hare (see above) leaving out the port and blood or one of these two.

Animals

Snail

A land mollusc rather than an animal but, for want of a better place, I have put it in this section. It is not generally known that all snails are edible and, since they are numerous, can constitute a copious food supply. However, much individual attention is required to prepare a snail for cooking and the larger ones repay the effort with greater dividends. There are three kinds of snail in Britain of which *Helix pomata* is the largest. It is said to have been introduced to Britain by the Romans expressly for eating. They kept them in special snail gardens surrounded by water to prevent their escape, fattening them up with all kinds of herbs and oatmeal. The other two kinds are the wood snail, *H. nemoralis*, and the garden snail, *H. aspersa*. All snails should be made to disgorge their last meal before cooking by putting them in a covered bucket full of salt water and changing the water several times over a period of 6 hours. Large snails are best cooked by the traditional recipe of *Escargots dit de Bourgogne* found in most cookery books. Smaller ones are probably better removed from their shells and stewed thus:

Escargots Petits Gris au Vin Rouge

Cover the snails with water, bring to the boil and simmer for 8 minutes. Then plunge them in cold water, remove from their shells, wash well and drain. Meanwhile put in an earthenware pan some diced streaky bacon, button onions, crushed garlic and good red wine. Add the snails, salt and pepper and a bouquet garni. Bring to the boil and cook in the oven very slowly for 2 hours. When cooked, a finishing-touch is to add a knob of butter kneaded into flour, and a liqueur-glass of brandy.

Hedgehog

Hedgehogs are found in most open country but, as they are a valuable animal, eating slugs and snails and other destructive insects, they should not be taken for food unless absolutely necessary or unless found dead, killed by a passing car. Hedgehogs were traditional gypsy food. They cooked them by wrapping the hedgehog in clay, then digging a hole in the ground, lining this with stones and lighting a wood fire on them. When a good bed of ashes had accumulated, the hedgehog was put in, covered with the ashes and left to cook. Once done the clay was broken with a sharp blow and the spines came away with the clay. Another method was to skin and gut the hedgehog first then roast it on a spit.

Grey Squirrel

Introduced into this country in 1876,

Hedgehog

Wrapped in clay

. . . cooked in hot ashes

their ability to adapt to all kinds of living conditions, from London parks to Scottish forests, has led to their proliferation at the expense of the indigenous red squirrel, now quite rare. A squirrel which has been feeding on the right ingredients can be as large, fat and sweet-tasting as a rabbit. One that has not can taste like bad curried chicken. However, casseroled in a good, strong, tasty sauce, even the rankest squirrel is made quite palatable and they are an abundant source of free food.

Sautéed Squirrel

Wash, wipe and quarter 2 squirrels. Rub with salt and pepper, slowly fry an onion and a crushed clove of garlic in some butter until golden. Add squirrel and 1 tablespoon chopped ham, sprinkle with flour and fry until brown. Then add $1\frac{1}{2}$ cups red wine, thyme, a bayleaf, 1 teaspoon grated lemon rind, cayenne pepper, salt and pepper. Simmer until tender.

Rat

Another form of vermin which, when they have been feeding on clean food, are considered, by those who have tried them, to be not bad at all. Gypsies frequently eat rats and anyone who has been in a state of siege, penury or imprisonment will be well acquainted with the taste. If ever you have the need to eat rat, it is best wrapped in bacon fat and slow roasted.

Spring and Summer Menus

Spring

All leaves begin to grow and nettles and stem vegetables are at their peak. Seaweed regenerates and morel mushrooms appear. Fish return to shores and rivers after their winter migrations but animals and birds are protected during their breeding season. It is the time to make flower wines from dandelion, may and coltsfoot.

Herb Soup

Melt 25g (1oz) butter in a pan, add 25g (1oz) flour and cook for 1 minute. Stir in 550ml (1pt) chicken stock and bring to the boil. Add 3 tablespoons herbs—caraway leaves, garlic mustard, mint, whatever is available—cover and simmer for 20 minutes. Taste, adjust seasoning, stir in 1 tablespoon fresh or sour cream, sprinkle with herbs and serve.

Mackerel Stuffed with Sorrel

Clean, bone and remove heads of 4 mackerel. Lay them flat on a board, skin side down. Melt 50g (2oz) butter in a pan and blend with 50g (2oz) fresh white breadcrumbs and 4 tablespoons chopped sorrel. Divide stuffing between fish and, starting at the head end, roll them up. Place the rolls close together in a baking dish, dot with butter and season. Pour over 2 tablespoons lemon juice, cover and bake in an oven 205 °C (400 °F) gas mark 6 for 30–35 minutes.

Cream Cheese with Ramsons
(eaten with oatcakes)

Make a cream cheese by setting aside some creamy milk until it goes sour and solid. Then pour into a muslin, hang in a cool place and leave to drip. When this has ceased, remove curd from muslin and mix with chopped ramson stalks, salt and pepper. Eat with oatcakes made by using the recipe on page 25).

Coltsfoot Wine

Dissolve 1.5kg (3½lb) sugar in 4.5l (1gal) water and bring to the boil. Simmer for 5 minutes, remove from heat and leave to cool. Add the rinds of

2 oranges and 2 lemons and 4.5l (1gal) coltsfoot flowers and stir well. Add previously activated yeast, cover and leave in a warm place to ferment for 7 days. Strain into a fermentation jar and insert an airlock. Leave until fermentation has ceased, then bottle.

Summer

Green vegetables such as cow parsnip, watercress, yarrow and hedge garlic, although they have lost their spring tenderness, are there in abundance. Thistles and samphire reach maturity. Earthnuts and chamomile are in flower as are elders in late June. Ash keys are ready for collection and pickling in early summer, oats later. Berries begin with raspberries and strawberries. Molluscs are in prime condition and fish and meat is in plentiful supply.

Shellfish Soup

Chop 1 large potato and 1 onion and cook gently in 25g (1oz) butter for a few minutes. Add 1.1l (2pt) shellfish, 1.4l (2½pt) fish stock or water, 2 crushed cloves of garlic, a bay leaf, parsley and a bunch of edible seaweed, fresh or dried. Bring to the boil and simmer until cooked. Remove the fish from their shells and return to the soup. Reheat, stir in 275ml (½pt) cream, sprinkle with chopped parsley and serve.

Jugged Pigeon

'Clean and remove the liver of 1 pigeon. Put the liver in cold water, bring to the boil, remove from the heat immediately and chop finely.
Stuffing : push the yolks of 2 hardboiled eggs through a sieve (reserve the whites) and add 1 cup fresh breadcrumbs, the chopped liver, 2 tablespoons mixed herbs and chopped parsley. Bind together with a beaten egg and season well with salt and pepper. Stuff the pigeon with this mixture and fasten with a toothpick.
To cook : put the pigeon in a casserole dish with 2 onions finely sliced and pour over 275ml (½pt) cider. Add bouquet garni and 275ml (½pt) stock. Bring to the boil. Bake in a slow oven for 1½–2½ hours until very tender. When cooked, tip off liquid into a saucepan through a sieve. Make up to 275ml (½pt) with extra stock if necessary. Add a large squeeze of lemon, thicken with arrowroot and bring to the boil. Put pigeon in a dish, pour over the gravy, sprinkle with finely chopped egg white, parsley and deep-fried croutons of bread.' Suki Kinloch.

Mint Sorbet

Boil 415ml (¾pt) water with 100g (4oz) sugar and the pared rind of 2 lemons for 5 minutes. Draw aside and add 1 large handful of mint leaves picked from their stalks. Leave to infuse for 10 minutes. Add strained lemon juice. Cool and freeze until firm. Serve covered with chopped mint.

Lime Blossom Wine

Dry 1.7l (3pt) lime blossom in the sun to bring out the flavour, then boil them in 4.5l (1gal) water for 30 minutes. When cool, add 450g (1lb) clean wheat, 450g (1lb) chopped raisins and 1.5kg (3½lb) sugar. Stir until sugar dissolves. Add some previously activated yeast, cover and leave to ferment for 3 weeks, strain and bottle. Keep, if possible, for 1 year before drinking.

Autumn and Winter Menus

Autumn

Nuts are ready for picking and storing. Fungi are at their best. Animals are fat from summer herbage and game-birds are in season. There are berries in abundance : blackberries, rowanberries, and elderberries. For vegetables, wood sorrel, ground elder and chickweed are still growing.

Mushrooms in Parsley and Garlic

Sprinkle a little olive oil over some mushrooms and leave to marinate— slice if large. Drain off any juice which has accumulated and fry them in fresh oil. After 5 minutes, add to every 225g ($\frac{1}{2}$lb) mushrooms 2 tablespoons parsley chopped with a little garlic and 2 tablespoons breadcrumbs. Stir. When the juices have absorbed the mixture, serve.

Rabbit Pie

'Joint rabbit and fry floured in a little butter. Remove and keep warm. Fry 2 rashers of bacon and 1 small onion in remaining fat. Add 1 dessertspoon flour, 275ml ($\frac{1}{2}$pt) stock, salt and pepper. Return joints to pan and cook gently for 1 hour. Put in a pie-dish and cover with shortcrust pastry made in the proportions of 100g (4oz) butter to 225g (8oz) flour. Bake for $\frac{1}{2}$ hour or until nicely brown on top.'
Pamela Urquhart.

Bilberry Sweet with Nuts

Cream 50g (2oz) butter with 2 egg yolks and 3–4 tablespoons sugar. Add 75–100g (3–4oz) wholemeal bread previously soaked in milk and 90g (3$\frac{1}{2}$oz) milled nuts. Add 250g (9oz) bilberries or any other berry of your choice. Fold in 2 whites of egg stiffly beaten. Butter a fireproof dish and bake in a medium oven for 30–40 minutes at 180 °C (350 °F) gas mark 4.

Blackberry Wine

Put 4.5l (1gal) blackberries in a large bowl and pour over 4.5l (1gal) boiling water. Cover and leave to stand for 7 days stirring daily. Strain through a muslin on to 1.8kg (4lb) sugar, stir well and add some previously activated yeast. Put into a fermentation jar and insert an airlock if possible, otherwise plug top with cotton wool. Leave to ferment to a finish. Bottle. Keep for at least 6 months before using.

Winter

Sloes and hawthorn have been tenderised by a few frosts and are ready for picking. Fungi last until December with the right weather. The seaweed laver is in season and there are root vegetables to be dug. Game-birds are in season until around Christmas. After this, there is a lean period during which time pickles, preserves, potted or salted meat are very welcome, until the first spring leaves start to appear in late February or early March, earlier in the very south.

Potted Eel

Remove skins, heads, tails and fins and open at the belly from the head down to the tail. Wash well, clean in salt water, and dry. Dust with flour. For 4.5kg (10lb) eel, prepare pickle of 35g (1½oz) bayleaves, 50g (2oz) marjoram, 25g (1oz) thyme, 675g (1½lb) baysalt, 225g (½lb) coarse sugar, 275ml (½pt) porter or beer. Cut up fish and lay in a deep dish with alternate layers of seasoning. Cover and leave for 24 hours, longer if the slices are thick. When thoroughly pickled, wash with salt water, dry, and dust with flour. Fry in hot oil until brown, drain and cool.

The next day, lay in pots and cover with clarified butter.

Wild Duck with Thyme Stuffing

Stuffing : mix together with 1 egg 225g (½lb) sausage meat, 1 finely chopped onion, 1 tablespoon chopped thyme, 2 tablespoons chopped parsley, salt and pepper. Stuff bird and cover with bacon and a buttery paper. Roast until cooked to your preference, about 1 hour.

Buttery Apple Crumble

Smear the bottom of a small pie-dish with butter. Slice apples and place in layers with more butter, sugar, cinnamon and cloves. Make a crumble with 100g (4oz) butter, 100g (4oz) sugar and 150g (6oz) flour. Put on top of apples and bake until the crumble is brown.

Sloe Wine

Pour 1.1l (2pt) boiling water over 1.1l (2pt) sloes and leave to stand for 4 days, stirring at least once every day. Strain and add to each 1.1l (2pt) liquid, 450g (1lb) sugar. Leave for another 4 days, stirring each day. Bottle after it has settled but do not cork tightly until it has finished working.

Food to Avoid

Nuts

There are no poisonous nuts in Britain. Identification book : see Plants.

Seaweed

Seaweeds as a species are like plants, generally dying down in winter and growing again in spring and, as with plants, the younger they are the better they taste. There are no poisonous varieties of seaweed growing in British waters.

Identification book : *Collins Pocket Guide to the Sea Shore*, J. Barrett and C. M. Yonge (Collins).

Fish

Except for jellyfish and some tropical species, there are no poisonous fish. However, once dead, fish deteriorate quickly and should always be eaten as fresh as possible. As a rule beware of fish with flabby skins, slimy gills and sunken eyes, fish that smell and dent permanently when pressed with a thumb.

Identification book : *Oxford Book of Vertebrates*, Marion Nixon and Derek Whiteley (OUP).

Molluscs

Edible throughout the year but best avoided during the breeding season— hence the saw advising against eating molluscs when there is an 'r' in the month. Not only does this ensure next year's supply of molluscs but they also taste inferior at this time. Since most bivalves—molluscs such as mussels with shells in two halves—feed by pumping water through themselves and filtering out the food particles, molluscs which live in dirty water, near human habitation or where sewage is pumped into the sea should be avoided. Dead molluscs decompose rapidly so always ensure that any you intend to eat are alive. Test this by prising open the shells a fraction ; if they snap shut again immediately, the mollusc is alive. If the shell is already open or fails to close, it is probably dead or dying and should be discarded.

Identification book : *Collins Pocket Guide to the Sea Shore*, J. Barrett and C. M. Yonge (Collins).

Animals

No animal is poisonous but they are composed, as we all are, of what they eat. Therefore any animal which is carnivorous or fed on inferior fodder will not have the juicy, sweet meat of one which has been eating good, succulent pasture.

Identification book : *Oxford Book of Vertebrates*, Marion Nixon and Derek Whiteley (OUP).

Birds

Although no birds are poisonous, like animals their meat is affected by their diet and this makes some, especially sea birds, rank and inedible. Study the diet of the bird and remember that it is this, recycled, which you will be eating.

Identification book : *A Field Guide to the Birds of Britain and Europe*, Peterson, Mountfort and Hollom (Collins).

Fungi

The golden rule with fungi is always to identify precisely before eating. There are several good guides ; the

Death cap

Destroying angel

Collins guide (see below) is an excellent one with a complete list of edible fungi. Our fear of fungi has led to the neglect of this enormous and rich source of food. Fungi you pick from the wild will have infinitely more flavour than any you can buy. Ninety per cent of deaths can be attributed to three fungi, the death cap *Amanita phalloides* (a greenish to cream-coloured cap and distinct volval ring, it grows in deciduous woods, especially beech and oak), its relation the destroying angel *Amanita virosa* (wholly white fungi with white gills, a volval ring and found in deciduous woods on poor soil) and the rare fool's mushroom, *Amanita verna*. There are also many others which are slightly poisonous or which tend to produce an allergy in certain people. Therefore, if it is a species which you have not tried before, eat a limited quantity first time. Identification book: *Collins Guide to Mushrooms & Toadstools*, Morten Lange and Bayard Hora (Collins).

Plants

All species of buttercup (*Ranunculus*) are poisonous as are all spurge (*Euphorbia*) and the two species of hellebore, *Helleborus foetidus* and *H. viridis*. Hemlock (*Conium maculatum*) was the deadly draught given to Socrates and deadly nightshade (*Atropa belladonna*) the source of belladona. Although the foxglove produces Digitalis, the drug used in the cure of heart diseases, it is poisonous in large quantitites. All the following are poisonous: columbine (*Aquilegia vulgaris*), baneberry (*Actaea spicata*), alder (*Frangula alnus*), buckthorn (*Rhamnus cathartica*), bittersweet (*Solanum dulcamara*), cowbane (*Cicuta virosa*), black nightshade (*Solanum nigrum*), spindle tree (*Euonymus europaeus*), monkshood (*Aconitum anglicum*), baneberry (*Actaea spicata*), privet (*Ligustrum vulgare*), mezereon, (*Daphne mezereum*), laurel (*Daphne laureola*), mistletoe (*Viscum album*), Ivy (*Hedera helix*), tubular water dropwort (*Oenanthe fistulosa*), hemlock water dropwort (*Oenanthe crocata*), fine-leaved water dropwort (*Oenanthe aquatica*), fool's parsley (*Aethusa cynapium*), white bryony (*Bryonia dioica*), dog's mercury (*Mercurialis perennis*), henbane (*Hyoscyamus niger*), thorn-apple (*Datura stramonium*), lily-of-the-valley (*Convallaria majalis*), fritillary (*Fritillaria meleagris*), meadow saffron (*Colchicum autmnals*), darnel rye-grass (*Lolium temulentum*), yew (*Taxus baccata*).

Identification books: *The Concise British Flora in Colour*, W. Keble Martin, Michael Joseph (Ebury Press). *Oxford Book of Flowerless Plants*, F. H. Brightman (OUP).

Further reading from David & Charles

GOOD FOOD GROWING GUIDE
Gardening and Living Nature's Way
John Bond and the Staff of 'Mother Earth'
A new-look growing guide to healthier and
happier living
241 × 148mm   illustrated

ECONOMY COOK BOOK
Mary Griffiths
A guide to how to cope with rising food and
housekeeping prices and still produce tasty
and nutritious meals
216 × 138mm

COST-EFFECTIVE SELF-SUFFICIENCY
or The Middle-Class Peasant
Eve and Terence McLaughlin
A practical guide to self-sufficiency, proving
that life as 'middle-class peasants' is not only
viable but enormously enjoyable and satisfying
247 × 171mm   illustrated

EAT CHEAPLY AND WELL
Brenda Sanctuary
Rising food prices make this up-to-the-
minute book a must for today's housewives
216 × 138mm   illustrated

GROWPLAN VEGETABLE BOOK
A Month-by-Month Guide
Peter Peskett and Geoff Amos
A practical, easy-reference guide to growing
super vegetables, and fruit too, month by
month
250 × 200mm   illustrated

GROWING FOOD UNDER GLASS:
1001 Questions Answered
Adrienne and Peter Oldale
An indispensable guide to setting up and
maintaining every kind of glasshouse,
together with an A–Z rundown of the familiar
and unusual fruit and vegetables to be grown
210 × 148mm   illustrated

GROWING FRUIT:
1001 Questions Answered
Adrienne and Peter Oldale
Answers all the questions a novice might ask
about pests and diseases, choice of tree
shapes and varieties, and pruning techniques
210 × 148mm   illustrated

GROWING VEGETABLES:
1001 Questioned Answered
Adrienne and Peter Oldale
All you need to know about growing
vegetables in a simple question and answer
format
210 × 148mm   illustrated

COMPLETE BOOK OF HERBS AND SPICES
Claire Loewenfeld and Philippa Back
A comprehensive guide to every aspect of
herbs and spices—their history and traditions.
cultivation, uses in the kitchen, and health and
cosmetics
242 × 184mm   illustrated

COOK OUT
Frances Kitchin
For the cook on a caravanning or camping
holiday, Frances Kitchin provides the answers
to all the problems when cooking meals with
the minimum of facilities
210 × 132mm   illustrated

British Library Cataloguing in Publication D

Urquhart, Judy
    Food from the wild. – (Penny pinchers).
    1. Plants, Edible – Great Britain   2. Animal
food
    I. Title   II. Series
    574.6'1   TX357

ISBN 0–7153–7545–8

© Judy Urquhart 1978

All rights reserved. No part of this
publication may be reproduced, stored
in a retrieval system, or transmitted,
in any form or by any means, electronic,
mechanical, photocopying, recording or
otherwise, without the prior permission
of David & Charles (Publishers) Limited

Set in Univers
and printed in Great Britain
by Redwood Burn Limited
for David & Charles (Publishers) Limited
Brunel House   Newton Abbot   Devon

Published in the United States of America
by David & Charles Inc
North Pomfret   Vermont 05053   USA

Published in Canada
by Douglas David & Charles Limited
1875 Welch Street   North Vancouver   BC